Cambridge Elements

Elements in Religion and Monotheism
edited by
Paul K. Moser
Loyola University Chicago
Chad Meister
Affiliate Scholar, Ansari Institute for Global Engagement with Religion, University of Notre Dame

MONOTHEISM AND CREATION

David Cheetham
University of Birmingham

CAMBRIDGE
UNIVERSITY PRESS

Shaftesbury Road, Cambridge CB2 8EA, United Kingdom

One Liberty Plaza, 20th Floor, New York, NY 10006, USA

477 Williamstown Road, Port Melbourne, VIC 3207, Australia

314–321, 3rd Floor, Plot 3, Splendor Forum, Jasola District Centre, New Delhi – 110025, India

103 Penang Road, #05–06/07, Visioncrest Commercial, Singapore 238467

Cambridge University Press is part of Cambridge University Press & Assessment, a department of the University of Cambridge.

We share the University's mission to contribute to society through the pursuit of education, learning and research at the highest international levels of excellence.

www.cambridge.org
Information on this title: www.cambridge.org/9781009571715

DOI: 10.1017/9781009357395

© David Cheetham 2025

This publication is in copyright. Subject to statutory exception and to the provisions of relevant collective licensing agreements, no reproduction of any part may take place without the written permission of Cambridge University Press & Assessment.

When citing this work, please include a reference to the DOI 10.1017/9781009357395

First published 2025

A catalogue record for this publication is available from the British Library

ISBN 978-1-009-57171-5 Hardback
ISBN 978-1-009-35741-8 Paperback
ISSN 2631-3014 (online)
ISSN 2631-3006 (print)

Cambridge University Press & Assessment has no responsibility for the persistence or accuracy of URLs for external or third-party internet websites referred to in this publication and does not guarantee that any content on such websites is, or will remain, accurate or appropriate.

For EU product safety concerns, contact us at Calle de José Abascal, 56, 1°, 28003 Madrid, Spain, or email eugpsr@cambridge.org

Monotheism and Creation

Elements in Religion and Monotheism

DOI: 10.1017/9781009357395
First published online: November 2025

David Cheetham
University of Birmingham

Author for correspondence: David Cheetham, d.cheetham@bham.ac.uk

Abstract: This Element discusses the idea of creation ex nihilo as an expression of monotheistic belief mainly with reference to Jewish and Christian traditions. It outlines the philosophical and theological discussion about monotheism and creation, considering key historical figures such as Philo, Irenaeus, Augustine, and Aquinas as well as contemporary thinkers. It reviews key topics such as divine sovereignty, the goodness of creation, pantheism, process, and feminist thinking on creation. It argues for creation ex nihilo over other models. In particular, it examines the notion of 'creaturehood' as an overlooked and under-developed dimension in contemporary debates about the relationship between created humanity and the one God. The doctrine of creation does not just address the question of origins, it also serves to affirm the finite or immanent aspects of life.

Keywords: monotheism, creation, origins, anthropology, createdness

© David Cheetham 2025

ISBNs: 9781009571715 (HB), 9781009357418 (PB), 9781009357395 (OC)
ISSNs: 2631-3014 (online), 2631-3006 (print)

Contents

1 Why Talk About Creation? 1

2 Creator and World 9

3 Createdness 34

   Epilogue 43

   References 47

1 Why Talk About Creation?

1.1 Past and Present Concerns

Examining the landscape of theology and religious studies, the idea of 'creation' as a category for religious reflection is one that is often fraught with controversy. So, one perception about the topic is that it involves effectively a rancorous dispute between evolutionists and creationists. In this sense, 'creation' can sound antiscientific to contemporary ears. However, in the West, especially, although the doctrine of creation has been generally neglected during the modern period, there has been renewed interest in the last few decades. The reasons for this are manifold. From a scientific perspective, astrophysical theories about the universe's origins have raised new questions about its ultimate causation and fine tuning. Thus, in the mid-twentieth century, astrophysicists were largely split between the Big Bang theory (first proposed in 1927 by Georges Lemaître) and proponents of the steady-state theory (championed initially by Fred Hoyle). Notwithstanding any new conundrums presented by the James Webb telescope, the Big Bang seems to constitute the majority consensus, but, if so, this immediately raises questions about what happened *before* the initial bang. Although on the face of it, this might seem to be a kind of confirmation for a creation *ex nihilo* (out-of-nothing) model, we have to be careful because creation *ex nihilo* is something more radical. It generates a monotheistic picture that advances the view that God, self-existent, without need or resistance, created a world without opposition, which added nothing to God, from absolutely nothing. No pre-existing matter, however unformed, exists co-eternally with God (which, according to critics, would lend matter a kind of God-like status). That this is not the same as the 'nothing' before the Big Bang is perhaps made clear by statements by some physicists about the qualities or the potential of the 'nothing' that could have brought about the initial explosion.[1] But here, the physicists' nothing sounds suspiciously like *something*, and creation *ex nihilo* is about God making something from *absolutely nothing*. This means that the fortunes of creation *ex nihilo* are not wedded to the fortunes of the Big Bang as a theory. So, we need to clarify the connection between creation as a theological category and scientific, observational theories of origins. In what follows, we shall be exploring creation as a theological category, looking mostly at Jewish and Christian traditions.

Setting aside the controversies about origins, one of the other reasons that talk about creation has come to the fore stems from contemporary anxieties about climate change and global warming. Such issues have given impetus

---

[1] See the discussion in Leidenhag 2020, 8–9. To take an example, when the prominent cosmologist Lawrence Krauss proposes that the universe 'could and plausibly did arise from a deeper nothing—involving the absence of space itself' (Krauss 2012, 183), he is simply not occupying the same ontological ground.

to a whole range of theologies of nature and critical reflection on human stewardship. Going even further, provoked by such issues, many commentators have challenged dualistic theologies and sought to present new expressions of creation or holistic spiritualities, or feminist reconstructions that advance embodied theologies. Our topic, monotheism and creation, is not just an abstract consideration about cosmogony; instead, it is about the value of creation itself and our part in it. Even so, it does not really concern a *manner* of engaging with nature, like the nineteenth-century romantic spiritualities of nature. Rather, when the focus is on monotheism, the weight of the discussion about God and creation addresses the nature of a *relationship*. How we configure that relationship affects what we are able (or perhaps are compelled) to say about a whole range of other things, theological and practical. In particular, if we think about the distinction between God and creation then the question of proper human limitations as a created being and the consequent shape of anthropology is brought into focus. In this connection, Oliver Davies urges us to think of the idea of divine creation as a move towards a 'generous and creative exploration of the *meaning* of the world' (Davies 2004, 4). Perhaps no longer captured solely by a vision for transcendence, we might once again be drawn to consider the value of immanent concerns.

However, perhaps too much immanence is problematic? So, a different kind of issue centres on whether creation should be prioritized by religion or is it, in fact, a distraction from more lofty spiritual goals? If we think of religion as being primarily concerned with categories like the transcendent, spirituality, mystical experience, or even prayer and worship, then creation can look more like an immanent concern or merely a passing moment towards a future hope. Another way of putting this is that religion is commonly associated with overcoming or transcending the world rather than indulging it. Our spiritual instincts look upwards to connect with what is extraordinary and deeply meaningful rather than a facile quotidian existence. Or else, there is a danger of blurring the distinction between the mundane and things which are meant to be 'set apart.' So, the dilemma faced when 'locating the ecstatic in the quotidian' is that this may render religion a 'meaningless category' (See Tweed 2015, 372–374). However, what all this potentially ignores is the existential category of *createdness,* which calls for caution about such dualisms. Or rather, the doctrine of creation is not just an assent to the idea that the world has been created *in the past* or even that it has a divine origin; it also provokes us to consider how religious experience connects with the material dimensions of our existence now.

Similarly, how we value creation is closely connected to our view of God's relation to the world. If our concept of creation does not extend beyond the question of origins, then it will likely look like a doctrine that is not relevant to the present or future. However, we shall see that the notion of creation *ex nihilo* serves to allow for the finite or immanent aspects of created life as a place to inhabit wholeheartedly, notwithstanding the eschatological hope of things to come. In addition to this, Christianity acknowledges 'createdness as the fundamental feature of all reality' (Schwöbel 2004, 172) and not an irrelevance or a passing moment. For the Roman Catholic thinker, Edward Schillebeeckx, the fact of human createdness represents a crucial context for theological reflection, and for Christians, even if creation is not front and centre in their minds, it underpins all their other beliefs (see Schillebeeckx 1990, 90). So, its chief purpose is to act as a backdrop for other doctrines, such as theological anthropology, the conditions of human freedom, the question of stewardship and ecology, or redemption and eschatology (Hardy 2003, 109). In addition to this, a new orientation is formed between our ordinary everyday engagements and our religious experiences. That is, ordinary engagements become theologically significant simply by evoking a doctrine of creation that becomes a placeholder that holds together our spiritual and ordinary perceptions. If this creational perspective is omitted, Oliver Davies argues that our language displays a demarcation in thought between the alleged vagueness (e.g., mysticism) of our spiritual references and the concrete clarity (e.g., science) of our ordinary experience and accounts of the world. The reason for this is that we have no sense of the world or ourselves *as created*, a sense that, if retrieved, might provide a natural bridge between our knowledge of God, or our spiritual talk, and our ordinary engagements with the world (Davies 2004, 5–6).

1.2 Creation and Foundational Thinking

Josef Pieper makes the striking claim that 'the doctrine of creation is the concealed but basic foundation of classical Western metaphysics' (Pieper 1957, 58). This emerges from his engagement with Thomas Aquinas (c.1225–1274) and his notion of Being as *creatura*. This is a basic ontological commitment that identifies Aquinas as a philosophical theologian as opposed to just a pure philosopher. That is, Aquinas starts with certain theological axioms that act to underscore how we see or frame everything, and, for him, creation is a fundamental starting point that should infuse all philosophical thinking. This has been described as Aquinas' 'hidden key' to his thinking about the philosophy of Being. So, apart from God the Creator, 'nothing exists which is not *creatura*', and 'this createdness determines entirely and all-pervasively the inner structure of the creature' (Pieper 1957, 53). There is the Creator, who is *wholly other*, and everything else (*creatura*), and *creatura* includes even transcendental 'concepts.' This may be seen as solely a Christian gloss on how we should interpret the world, but the question is, how influential has this idea been on Western thinking? If we abstract the meaning of creation for a moment and translate it into terms like 'the ground', or 'foundations', then perhaps there are concomitants to be found in the philosophical and scientific search for fundamentals or priorities in thought. Or else, there is a deeper question about how the idea of creation, or foundations, is somehow wired into our intellectual subconscious. This is something that David Burrell picks out of Pieper's Thomistic reflections and suggests that creation as a 'foundation' has never wholly disappeared from Western thinking; instead, Burrell sees its recurrence in the philosophical quest for certainties and solid grounds. Nevertheless, it is not at all clear if this can be applied to the present zeitgeist, and indeed, the alleged freedom of *post*-modernism and its rebellion against the tyranny of metanarratives indicate that a different mood now prevails. Foundationalism may have peaked. However, post-modernism has a rather narrow target in that it sets itself against a particular kind of hard rationalist or Enlightenment foundationalism, and Burrell speculates that the contrasting idea of a personal and 'more flexible and subtle "foundation" in a free creator' (Burrell 2013, 6) may be appealing to the postmodern sensibility. Whilst we might be sceptical about this, one of the more profound aspects of the notion of a 'free creator' is that it reframes the idea of a *foundation* not as something arrived at by a rationalist or moral deduction as such, but as a pure 'gift.'

However, is creation something that must be, either explicitly or implicitly, a *theological* foundation? It seems to be Aquinas' viewpoint that we cannot ground creation in a neutral naturalism; or rather, creation is not just about marveling at nature in all its variety and spectacle, instead its peculiar character and purpose is defined by its relatedness to God as a created being. In short, the creational viewpoint is fideistic and revealed to the eyes of faith. Creation is *seeing-as* (Wittgenstein). Robert Jenson follows this line of reasoning when he argues that 'creation' is not something that can be assumed to be a common experience with the 'otherwise unbelieving' (Jenson 2004, 20). If we take this a step further, it means that when confessed as a *doctrine*, the topic of creation connects to further beliefs about the human condition, purpose, and redemption that a simple appeal to the natural order may not exhibit by itself. So, the doctrine of creation is 'credal in form' (Gunton 1997, 141). It is not a liminal space or a neutral platform. Instead, it is part of a basic confession of faith like the common Christian creed: 'I believe in God the Father, Maker of Heaven and Earth', or the Muslim confession stated in the Qur'an: 'He is God, the Creator, the Maker, the Shaper' (59.24). In Christian teaching, there is a cosmic statement about Christ: 'in him all things hold together' (Col.1:17), which makes it explicit that creation cannot be understood by Christians without a Christological reference. In fact, this latter verse has been cited in support of a more panentheistic interpretation, but we shall return to this later.

1.3 Creation and Shared Experience

Nevertheless, it is also true to say that creation is universal and public – it refers to all things. Thus, even though he wishes to highlight the specifically theological location that creation inhabits, Jenson nonetheless seeks to find some kind of universal concern. He suggests that all of humanity shares the pressing question about our ultimate origins (why are we here?) and the fact of existence, not just about what something is, but *that* it is. This is the sheer mystery of existence and the fact of things, the beginning of philosophical enquiry and wonder (Jenson 2004, 20). Similarly, Heidegger described an experience of 'thrown-ness' (*Geworfenheit*) – the feeling of being thrown into the world. Thus, there is a common human question about the fact of existence that one does not need the insight of faith to acquire. In this sense, the question of our origins is a public concern that is shared by believing and unbelieving alike.

Such talk about the sheer marvel or wonder of existence *itself* opens another topic that needs to be addressed, and this is what creation means apart from any past or future concerns. That is, can we look at creation itself apart from thinking about grand purposes or destinies? This concerns a contested idea of something categorically distinctive about creation that sets it apart from other redemptive or eschatological doctrines (for a critique, see Wilson 2013). Contested because, for many religious thinkers or theologians, creation should not be separated from these bigger themes. However, in an influential two-volume study called *Eccentric Existence* (2009), David Kelsey emphasizes precisely this point and does so by drawing attention to the creation account in the Wisdom literature in the Bible rather than that found solely in the Genesis narratives. The Genesis account connects creation with notions of fall and redemption, but the Wisdom texts seem to inhabit the immediate moments of everyday life. Thus, whereas the Genesis account has themes of fall and redemption that overlay the creation narrative, Kelsey argues that 'Wisdom's view of creation is conceptually separated from ideas of both reconciliation and eschaton':

> Wisdom's theology of creation is conceptually independent of that pattern of thought and is not shaped by any understanding of God's active relating to reconcile creatures from the estranging effects of sin and evil. Consequently,

in canonical Wisdom literature, stories of God relating to create are told for their own sake and are told in ways that do not bend their narrative logic (Kelsey 2009, 162).

Likewise, some scholars have observed that there is a lack of explicit reference to the redemptive story of Israel in the Wisdom literature, and this makes it difficult to appropriate its purpose beyond simply its wise sayings (See Zimmerli 1964, 146–158).[2] In addition, there are aspects of Biblical wisdom that can be found in other cultures, and this may suggest that such literature represents a more universal creational language. If so, there is an opportunity to say something important about the value of everyday wisdom as a dimension of *createdness* that takes us beyond overtly Biblical narratives. Because it cannot be simply reduced to the kinds of doctrines with which creation is often intimately connected (the beginning of things, fall, and redemption), it can be described as having a specific kind of reality. By 'reality' we are not making a simple identification with matter itself, or the material dimension, but speaking about the immediacy of everyday experience that occupies the present moment.

Nevertheless, even if we seek to isolate createdness as a unique domain, we cannot ignore the bigger context. The phenomenology of the finite world may be a useful place to consider the existential aspects of created life, but the theological task requires that the whole picture must be taken into account. Thus, if we widen the theological frame, there is a crucial question about the relationship between protology and eschatology. Are these things distinct, or do they form parts of a whole? This is hardly a new question, and it draws into it the related issue about how we see the role of time and history in the creation story. Is creation an instantaneously accomplished event, or does it involve progression and development? A prominent example of the latter is an important figure from the early Greek Christian tradition, St Irenaeus (c.130–202 CE), who is well-known for his two-stage account of the creation of humanity (*imago dei* and *similitudo dei*), where creation is perceived as something that envelops soul-making and redemption:

> All created things which through the bountiful goodness of God receive increase and persist on and on, shall gain the glory of the Eternal, for God bestows what is good without stint [. . .] The eternal is perfect, and this is God. Man has first come into being, then to progress, and by progressing come to manhood, and having reached manhood to increase, and thus increasing to persevere, and by persevering be glorified, and thus see his Lord (Irenaeus 1990, 68).

---

[2] For a good critique of Zimmerli, see Weeks 2016, 3–23.

Likewise, Gregory of Nyssa (c. 335 – c. 394) speaks of God's purpose as 'one, and one only; it is this: when the complete whole of our race shall have been perfected from the first man to the last.' In this sense, the creation and the end of all things are, as the Orthodox theologian David Bentley Hart puts it, a 'single science' (Hart 2019, 68). Creation becomes the whole of history viewed as a totality where all things are brought into full completion.

This is where the doctrine of creation becomes intertwined with the problem of evil and suffering. Should we consider moments of suffering as self-contained events in time, or do we take an overarching perspective on history and sweep such moments up into a future where everything is made good in the end? A contrasting view would be to look back to a perfect creation in the past that has gone wrong. Augustine expresses things this way (in contrast to Irenaeus):

> Human nature was certainly originally created blameless and without any fault; but the human nature by which each one of us is now born of Adam requires a physician, because it is not healthy. All the good things, which it has by its conception, life, senses, and mind, it has from God, its creator and maker. But the weakness which darkens and disables these good natural qualities, as a result of which that nature needs enlightenment and healing, did not come from the blameless maker but from original sin, which was committed by free will (Augustine 1995, 219).

This is a classic difference in approach to creation and its relationship to evil– the Augustinian and the Irenaean (See Hick 2007 [1966]). However, creation *ex nihilo* makes the problem of evil potentially more acute because it presents a picture of an all-powerful God who creates freely and without resistance. That is, there is nothing to be overcome as such (like a primordial chaos) that might go some way towards providing an explanatory framework for evil and its persistence. If this is the case, then where do we go intellectually with suffering and its explanation and final resolution? David Bentley Hart has picked this up and argues strongly that the moral meaning of creation *ex nihilo* must join up protology with eschatology to result in universal salvation for all. For Hart, 'the end of all things is their beginning, and only from the perspective of the end can one know what they are, why they have been made, and who God is . . . ' (Hart 2019, 68). Creation *ex nihilo* makes the problem of evil insurmountable if the end result for some people is an eternal hell. In fact, not to advocate for *ex nihilo* is an easier option because 'if [Christians] thought God a being limited by some external principle or internal imperfection, or if they were dualists, or dialectical idealists, or what have you – the question of evil would be an aetiological query only for them, not a terrible moral conundrum' (89–90). Because God creates out of total freedom and without opposition, then it is simply morally unthinkable, claims Hart, for there to be an 'irreconcilable remainder left behind' in the eschaton (71). Such an entailment would have to have been freely permitted – by definition (according to the *ex nihilo* view) unopposed by any force or will, and this is Hart's crucial point: 'Anything willingly done is done toward an end; and anything done toward an end is defined by that end' (68). So, God's very identity – God's goodness and moral character – is defined by the ends of creation. Hell's existence would imply that God is a 'failed creator'.

Notwithstanding the clamour of objections to Hart's position (and both academic and popular journals are crammed with them), we should note that the power of his position is built upon the implications of the creation *ex nihilo* model, in particular. If creation is a pure gift and creation occurs without necessity by a God who, in simplicity, is ontologically distinct from creation and who requires no addition, then arguments that depend on the alleged recalcitrance of the created order if things go awry do not appear to be very cogent ultimately. Nevertheless, Hart's instincts sound rather gnostic (there is very little from the Hebrew Bible in his *All Shall be Saved*), and despite the moral authority of his stance, another Orthodox theologian, Andrew Louth, 'wonders if he is defending a position with weapons that have no business here' (Louth 2020, 235). Hart seems impatient with any final appeal to mystery, creaturely independence, or the inscrutableness of divine fiat because 'in this divine outpouring there is no element of the "irrational": nothing purely spontaneous, or organic, or even mechanical, beyond the power of God's rational freedom' (Hart 2019, 71).

Doing justice to this particular discussion is beyond the scope of this book. However, the problem of evil is undoubtedly an important factor in how the relationship between God and creation is described. This issue is expressed variously by thinkers reflecting on creation and its meaning, ranging from liberationist or feminist theologians to those who reject creation *ex nihilo* and contest traditional accounts of God, such as process theologians. Process theology presents a model in which God indeed appears constrained by 'external principles' and operates as the chief power working to persuade creation to overcome evil. We shall say more about this in what follows.

To summarize, our discussion in this short book is concerned with creation as a theological or religious category rather than scientific theories about origins. Moreover, even though worries about climate change and the environment are rising up the cultural and political agenda, we will not be addressing these topics directly but rather focusing on the relationship between creation and monotheism through mostly Jewish and Christian sources. Even so, a consideration of creation is bound to turn our attention towards the nature of creaturehood and how this forces us to reconsider the relationship between transcendence and immanence as well as the goals of human life. Although creation relates to a primal universal concern about origins (why are we here?), there is an important sense that it is a kind of theological seeing-as. For example, when the Psalmist says 'The heavens are telling the glory of God, and the firmament proclaims his handiwork' (19.1) we could say that this is simply a species of a more universal sense of wonder at the fact that anything exists at all; or alternatively it is bound up with a credal assent (e.g. 'God created the world') such that its glory is a *gift* to those who believe. However, whatever we say about this, it is undeniable that there are many common experiences of the world that are shared by all, such as evil and suffering. Moreover, it is this experience that has been crucial for many thinkers trying to make sense of creation and its meaning. Thus, to what extent should the various models of creation account for this experience? Should those who propose them be conscious of the implications for theodicy, for example, or are there other, more axiomatic questions about existence *itself* that have priority? These are some of the questions that will occupy us in the next section.

2 Creator and World

We are not only concerned with cosmogony, but also with the consequences of the models of creation we follow. On the one hand, some models – like the *process* model – will present creation as a kind of long-term labour by God (with the co-operation of creation) to subdue the powers of chaos. Others will think in terms of creation *ex nihilo*. Or rather, creation as a gift without necessity or any difficulty, creation out of nothing. Perhaps more fundamentally, our ideas about creation are inextricably connected to what we think about God. Stated in its most basic form, Jewish, Christian, and Muslim monotheisms believe that reality's most ultimate category is one God—an all-powerful, all-knowing, benevolent reality that is the explanation and cause of everything apart from itself. Alongside more formal philosophical matters about divine causation, knowledge, or power, the very sense of what we think the category of 'God' implies is crucial to how we describe the specific relationship God has with creation. For example, Janet Soskice says just this sort of thing when she says 'creatio *ex nihilo* is not a teaching about the cosmos but about God' (Soskice 2021, 38). To be clear, she is speaking about a particular model of creation – *ex nihilo* – which emerged historically in Jewish and Christian thinking around the time of Second Temple Judaism (c.516 BCE – 70 CE) and the first few centuries of the Christian Church as a result of a theological and philosophical reflection on God's aseity.

If, as Soskice says, creation *ex nihilo* is about God, then what we say about how a monotheistic conception of God relates to creation is about how God acts right now and not just in the past. Put another way, creation *ex nihilo* describes a relationship more than a timeline. This might be contrasted with the deistic view that God has simply set things in motion at the beginning and left the machine to run by itself, so to speak. Another issue is that we might think that God is so *wholly other* to the world that no relationship to the world can be meaningfully described, and, if so, we run into conceptual difficulties if we also wish to imagine a God who is constantly intervening, re-fashioning, directing, providing, and so on. Viewed from the other direction, does creation affect God, or is God unchanged by the comings and goings of people, animals, climates, planets, and stars?

2.1 Out-of-Nothing

Creation *ex nihilo* is one of the most important doctrinal formulations (though by no means universally accepted). I say 'formulation' to indicate that it is not stated explicitly or directly in the scriptural traditions and has instead emerged historically out of the crucible of philosophical and theological dispute. On the other hand, many Jewish and Christian theologians believe that the credentials of creation *ex nihilo* have a clear implication within the Bible (and it is also present in the Qur'an).[3] Again, Soskice claims that creation *ex nihilo* is a 'scripturally driven piece of Christian metaphysics' (Soskice 2021, 40), though this is something that is not drawn necessarily from texts like Genesis 1 but rather from scripture as a whole. So, in the Hebrew Bible, the main sources are, alongside the Genesis account, the Psalms, Isaiah 40–55, and the wisdom literature (see Clifford 2021).

In one of the most famous passages, Genesis begins with this:

> 'In the beginning God created the heavens and the earth. The earth was without form and void, and darkness was upon the face of the deep; and the Spirit of God was moving over the face of the waters' (Gen 1:1–2 RSV)

Here, ostensibly, the passage does not appear to offer resounding support for creation *ex nihilo* because, taken by itself, verse 2 may be saying that there was a formless void already there that was then forged by God. However, the verse is not necessarily incompatible with an *ex nihilo* perspective, and one must

---

[3] Consider Q 52:35–36: 'Were they created from nothing, or were they the creators [of themselves]? Did they create the heavens and the earth? No! They do not have faith;' and 6.73: 'It is He who created the heavens and the earth in truth. On the day when he utters "Be", and it is, His utterance is the truth'; 24.25: He 'creates whatever He will.' (I am grateful to one of the reviewers of this book for bringing these to my attention).

recognize that such texts are not offered as statements that are meant to be parsed with philosophical rigour. Additionally, although a critic of creation *ex nihilo*, the Jewish biblical scholar Jon Levenson draws our attention to an important feature of the Genesis text. He notes the fact that there appears to be 'no active opposition to God's creative labor. He works on inert matter. In fact, rather than creation *ex nihilo*, "creation without opposition" is a more accurate nutshell statement of the theology underlying our passage' (Levenson 1994, 122).[4] Although Levenson draws some parallels between the Genesis account and Near Eastern traditions, this 'creation without opposition' is something distinctive about the Genesis view that would seem to suggest that the 'waters' in verse 2 are hardly an obstruction to God's action. Nevertheless, Levenson's argument takes place in the context of his reflections on the persistence of evil, and his narrative oscillates (frustratingly) between the forces of chaos, which allegedly throw into doubt God's plan, and God's triumph over such forces. Thus, he argues that the story of the Flood and passages like Ps. 74:12–17; Ps 104: 6–9 and Job 38:8–11 speak of God holding back, or containing, the world and its forces. These passages appear to share in the ancient world's 'combat myth of creation'. Moreover, although the Flood story includes a covenantal promise, it also ushers in a 'profound anxiety' at the precariousness of creation (14–15).

Nevertheless, many passages in the Bible appear to speak radically about God's transcendence. In fact, it is such statements that, in the period of Second Temple Judaism, cause key Jewish thinkers to advance proto *ex nihilo* ideas. So, many biblical statements do not present God as one who stands in oppositional relation to lower recalcitrant matter, or any contrarian force, but as one who is above all and to whom nothing can be *compared* (Ps. 113.5; Is.40.8). God is above all (2 Chron.2.6; Ps.97.9). God is not encumbered by the world and stands in relation to it as its Saviour and Judge (Is.33.22); God cannot be replaced by things or objects (Is.42.8; Hab.2:18). We find in the sixth century BCE a statement in Isaiah 40: 12–28 which sets out transcendent monotheism: 'To whom then will you liken God, or what likeness compare him? (vs 18)'; likewise, Isaiah 45.5 'I am the Lord, and there is no other, besides me there is no god.'[5] In 2 Maccabees, a deuterocanonical diasporic text from the second century BCE, a mother speaks to her son, saying: 'So I urge you, my child, to look at the sky and the earth. Consider everything you see there, and realize that God made it all from nothing, just as he made the human race.' (7.28). Again, this short passage is not a philosophical text, but it nevertheless exhibits what might be called the confident faith that is linked to creation *ex nihilo*. That is, the mother has assurance that God has the freedom and the power to

---

[4] See also chapter 5 of Levenson 1994.   [5] see also Isaiah 43:10ff; 44:8,23ff; 45:5f.22.

act supremely, as we might think when we 'look at the sky and the earth.' When we move ahead in time a few centuries to the Christian New Testament, we find similar affirmations, such as 'the God who gives life to the dead and calls into being things that were not.' (Rom. 4.17); and linked with exaltation: 'You are worthy, our Lord and God, to receive glory and honor and power, for you created all things, and by your will they were created and have their being' (Rev 4.11).

This brings into the foreground the confessional dimension of our inquiry. For some, like the mother in 2 Maccabees above, the fact that God is supreme over all is a source of great comfort and strength. In which case, we might say that creation *ex nihilo* represents a formal articulation of just such faith. However, for others, as we perhaps see in writers like Levenson and process or feminist writers (see later), creation *ex nihilo* gets in the way of trying to embrace a God who is embedded in the world or who shows solidarity with the struggle against chaos and evil.

However, returning to the scriptural texts, even if we cannot find explicit or philosophically watertight statements in scripture to support the *ex nihilo* position, this does not mean that it should not be inferred as a scriptural viewpoint. Or, even if certain scriptural passages ostensibly appear to express the idea of God forging creation from pre-existing matter, we must not necessarily take such statements in isolation from the totality of the scriptural testimony. In fact, such passages may simply exhibit the limitations of language when it comes to speaking about an act as profound and unfathomable as divine creation. So, if we go back to Genesis, we ought not to interpret certain verses (such as Gen 1.2) *prima facie* according to ancient comparisons but ask what kind of wider truth is being presupposed in scripture and tradition when we consider God's agency in creation. When narrating creation, scriptural writers were restricted by the limitations of the language of 'making'. Herein lies the difficulty in trying to describe the unique distinction between God and creation. How could a human writer accurately narrate the *impossible*? This is an argument made by David Burrell, who points out that when we describe the actions of a creator, we find it difficult to avoid 'presupposing something to work with'. If we fail to take account of such limitations, Burrell thinks 'we would never think creator except as demiurge' (Burrell 1994, 25).[6] In the end, it is a question of whether a total reading of scriptures makes accounts of God subduing recalcitrant pre-existent matter a likely interpretation. The scriptural texts, taken as a whole, speak of a God who is far above all things. So, whatever the textual ambiguities that exist in certain places, we have to ask if a 'demiurge' really fits when we consider such New Testament passages as 'I am the Alpha

---

[6] Burrell's immediate context here is the Islamic tradition, and his response to O'Shaughnessy's (1985) claim that *ex nihilo* is not explicit in the Qur'ānic texts.

and the Omega, the First and the Last, the Beginning and the End' (Rev 22.13)? Or 'Through him all things were made; without him nothing was made that has been made' (Jn 1.3). Though philosophy is clearly not the 'genre' of such texts, Burrell argues that later philosophical resolutions in the direction of *ex nihilo* were natural follow-ups that reflect the total commitment to monotheism in the faith of these traditions.

2.2 Ex nihilo, nihil fit?

Looking at the historical relationship between monotheism and creation, one of the most fundamental disputes centres around whether or not something can come from nothing. For much of the ancient world, and for the Greeks in particular, the predominant view was that the gods worked to subdue chaos and fashion pre-existent matter. The idea that something could come from nothing was not entertained. Famously, Parmenides in the sixth century BCE stated, '*ex nihilo, nihil fit*' (nothing comes from nothing). However, the history of thought concerning monotheism (in the Abrahamic traditions) gradually came to the view that the sovereignty of God needed to be stated in much stronger terms.

Stepping back for a moment, we might take the account offered by Plato (c.427–348 BCE) in the *Timaeus* as a milestone text for the classical Greek view:

> This is in the truest sense the origin of creation and of the world, as we shall do well in believing on the testimony of wise men: God desired that all things should be good and nothing bad, so far as this was attainable. Wherefore also finding the whole visible sphere not at rest, but moving in an irregular and disorderly fashion, out of disorder he brought order, considering that this was in every way better than the other (Plato 1892, 450).

We can see how one rendering of Gen.1.2 – God forming the world from pre-existent matter – might be perceived to be coincident with Plato's *Timaeus*. However, in light of our comments in the previous section, there is a question about whether the 'God above all' can really be said to align with the sense in the *Timaeus* that the Creator has brought order from chaos, 'so far as this was attainable.' Nevertheless, there is a certain question begging here – as process thinkers would undoubtedly point out.

So, where does creation *ex nihilo* come from? Not, as it seems, from the classical Greek context that influenced, for example, Second Temple Judaism and the early Christian Church. In fact, in the latter case, it emerges as an explicit philosophical movement in response to the challenge of Gnostic teaching in the second century CE. Gerhard May, in his account of the rise of creation *ex nihilo* in the Second Temple period, notes that 'more books were written by Jews about the agreement between Judaism and Greek philosophy than vice versa' (May 2006, 435). This was largely because of the desire to give Jewish ideas philosophical credibility. In doing so, Jewish thinkers adopted the language of the Greeks and perhaps absorbed much of their philosophy about monotheism as well. But as time progressed, the Platonic picture of the divine ordering of chaos and the making of the world from pre-existing materials did not sit well with the monotheism of Jewish and Christian thinkers, even if they found it difficult to fully separate themselves from it.

We see this most notably in the work of the Jewish philosopher, Philo of Alexandria (c.20 BCE – 50 CE). Philo is a significant figure in our discussion about monotheism and creation because he appears to come tantalizingly close to the idea of creation *ex nihilo* but is reluctant ultimately to resist the idea of the eternity of matter that is present, as we have seen, in the example of the *Timaeus* above. Philo attempted to connect the biblical notions of creation with Greek ideas. He is in no doubt about the transcendence and omnipotence of God and, in this sense, his ideas tend to favour the biblical notion rather than Plato's creator. Key statements from Philo's writings indicate this: '[God] is full of Himself and sufficient for Himself. It was so before the creation of the world and is equally so after the creation of all that is. He cannot change or alter and needs nothing else at all, so that all things are Him but He Himself in the proper sense belongs to no one' (Philo 1989, 4.27). In other places, Philo speaks of God creating space and time. Nevertheless, May argues that Philo did not fully state that God creates from nothing in any developed ontological sense, nor did he directly contradict the prevailing Hellenistic ideas of the eternity of matter (see May 2006, 437–439).

If we turn to early developments in the Christian church, two voices stand out as supporters of creation *ex nihilo*, Irenaeus (c. 130 – c. 220 CE) and Theophilus of Antioch (d.185 CE).[7] Speaking against second century Gnostics like Valentinus and Marcion (though the latter was actually very critical of Gnostic sophistry), Irenaeus contrasts human creativity with divine creation:

> To attribute the substance of all things that were created to the power and the will of the God of all things is credible and acceptable, and stable. In this regard, one might well say: What is impossible with mortals is possible with God. The reason for this is that men and women cannot make anything out of nothing, only out of matter that exists; God, however, is far superior to humankind inasmuch as he himself invented the matter of his work, since previously it did not exist (Irenaeus 2012, 36–37).

---

[7] For a detailed account, see McFarland 2014, 1–15.

Around the same time, though perhaps with not as much philosophical sophistication as other early voices,[8] Theophilus of Antioch exhibits his radical monotheism in a key statement about God's sovereignty:

> He has no beginning, because he is uncreated; he is immutable because he is immortal. He is called God because he established everything on his own steadfastness (Ps.103:5) and because he runs; the word 'run' means to run and set in motion and energize and nourish and provide and govern everything alive. He is Lord because he is master of the universe, Father because he is before the universe, Demiurge and Maker because he is creator and maker of the universe, Most High because he is above everything, Almighty because he controls and surrounds everything [...] God made everything out of what did not exist (2 Macc.7.28) ... (Theophilus of Antioch 1970)

In both these statements, we see a keen advocacy for what might have seemed indefensible to religious philosophers of the day – something coming from 'what did not exist'. However, perhaps what made things even less palatable (and which contrasted with the prevailing assumptions of the time) is the idea that creation is 'very good' (Gen 1:31). According to the Platonic view, the world of matter is imperfect and subject to constant change and decay. Perfection is more likely to be found in the spiritual realm. Thus, the assertion that creation is 'very good' is a discordant idea. Indeed, it would have jarred with prominent docetics like Marcion (85–160 CE), who rejected the Hebrew scriptures in favour of a transcendental good God, the high God, unsullied by the evil of matter, and who seeks through faith in Christ to save people from the world of the 'creator' god. Irenaeus lambasted Marcion for his 'two gods' scenario because ' ... if there is anything outside of [God], then he is no longer the Fullness of all things, and he does not contain all things, because whatever they say is outside of him will be lacking to the Fullness or to the God who is above all things' (Irenaeus 2012, 17). Nevertheless, even if we acknowledge fundamental problems with his dualistic system, Marcion's basic intuition that the world is an evil place raises nagging questions that we should take seriously. Marcion's aversion to it might seem entirely reasonable to many who experience acute suffering or disaster and find it hard to reconcile these things with the idea of a good Creator. In fact, it was the horrors of existence that caused the great pessimistic philosopher of the Nineteenth century, Arthur Schopenhauer, to pour scorn on what he saw as the delusion of the 'good world': 'we have not to be pleased but rather be sorry about the existence of the world' (Schopenhauer 2008, 576) he writes, and 'everywhere in nature we see contest,

---

[8] See Robert Grant's reference to Eusebius' remark about Theophilus as 'elementary' in his introductory essay (Theophilus of Antioch 1970, ix).

struggle, and the fluctuation of victory ... Every grade of the will's objectification fights for the matter, the space, and the time of another ... ' (146). Put simply, when we consider creation and monotheism together, it brings into sharp focus the problem of evil. In this sense, Marcion's dualism might be seen as an attempt to set God apart from the horror of creation and effectively create an incorruptible sanctuary for truth and goodness. However, in the end, a commitment to monotheism means that we cannot find such a convenient escape. We are therefore tasked with not only giving an account of the power of God but also of God's intentions towards the creation. This has resulted in a wide range of responses from theologians. For example, in terms of divine power, we shall see in a moment that one influential movement, known as process thought, rejects the notion of *ex nihilo* and instead opts for the (quasi-*Timaean*) view of God working to persuade the creation towards a good outcome.

Contra figures like Marcion, one of the main distinctions that were made during the early Christian period was the affirmation of the material order as good; indeed, contrary to Gnostic beliefs, the Nicene Creed (325 CE) states that God is not just the author of some higher transcendent realm, but the 'maker of heaven and earth'. Moreover, Jewish, Christian (and later, Islamic) scholars came to the view that the position most consistent with their scriptural traditions was that God created out of nothing. Nevertheless, the Platonic distinction between a 'lower' world of matter and the 'higher' worlds of spirit, mind, and intellect underpins a powerful current in the Western religious mind that tends to speak of the inherent value of created material existence only *sotto voce*. This forces us to revisit the question of the meaning and value of creation in itself and our createdness. Is there a danger that creation is perceived to be a lower reality that will be ultimately discarded by the eschatological consummation to come? Indeed, it is this kind of thinking that may end up adding grist to complaints like Lynn White's protest about the alleged 'ecologic effects' of believing that 'the saint is not in natural objects; he may have special shrines, but his citizenship is in heaven' (White 1967, 1207). So, affirming both the unnecessary giftedness of creation and its inherent goodness (apart from redemptive and eschatological themes) goes some way towards shifting the focus on how we interpret creation and its purposes both in the present and the future.

2.3 Emanation

Another prominent theme that is found in the history of thinking about monotheism and creation is concerned with the overflow or superabundance of God. Here, we have to distinguish between the voluntary and involuntary forms of this. The former case we have already spoken about in terms of the idea of God's unnecessary gift of creation from nothing. The latter can be found in the other versions of Platonism that continued well into the Third century CE, such as the Neoplatonic philosopher, Plotinus (204–70 CE). Plotinus is a classic representative of emanationism, in which the world is considered to be a 'great chain of being' that proceeds from the One, rather like the brightness of the sun diminishing incrementally as one moves further away. At first glance, this appears to be fully consistent with the superabundance of God that has gratuitously exceeded its boundaries. Indeed, such an affinity seems manifestly justified when we read from Plotinus' second treatise of Book V of his *Enneads*: 'The One, perfect because it seeks nothing, has nothing, and needs nothing, overflows, as it were, and its superabundance makes something other than itself' (Plotinus 1984, 59).

However, there are important aspects of Plotinus' vision that are different in emphasis. Firstly, it seems that creation is an inevitable aspect of God (as if it follows God around!). That is, emanation is a necessary property of God. This is brought out in a few other statements made in the *Enneads*. So: 'The One is all things and not a single one of them: it is the principle of all things, not all things, but all things have that other kind of transcendental existence; for in a way they do occur in the One; or rather they are not there yet, *but they will be*' (59).[9] Again, in Plotinus' chain of being, what follows the One is the One-Many (see 143) and this seems to proceed irresistibly from the One: 'How then could the most perfect, the first Good, remain in itself as if it grudged to give itself or was impotent, when it is the productive power of all things' (143). And, even further, 'something must certainly come into being from it', and 'that it is from it that they come is absolutely necessary' (145).

As we have said, what such statements imply is that Plotinus' emanation system is a necessary aspect of God. A more formal term to describe the character of the relationship between God and creation might therefore be *creatio ex deo* and, as we can see, this potentially conflicts with the idea of the absolute sovereignty of God because creation becomes an involuntary act ('necessary emanation', Burrell 2004, 211) or an inherent aspect of the divine being rather than something that has taken place as a completely voluntary, unnecessary and free act. So, although theologians may rightly consider it important to speak of creation as an overflow of divine love or as a gratuitous gift, it remains a wholly free act, without compulsion or necessity. Simply the result of God's sovereign choice.

---

[9] Emphasis mine.

Neoplatonic influences also played a significant role in the development of classical Islamic thought about creation, and these thinkers had an important influence on Christian scholasticism in the Middle Ages and on the work of Aquinas. Some of them supported a more emanationist Neoplatonic view, others the *ex nihilo* view. For example, the ideas of emanation gained prominence especially in the work of two influential early Islamic philosophers, al-Fārābī (d.950 CE) and Ibn Sīnā (d.1037 CE). Although significant and sophisticated, their ideas were controversial and were criticized by al-Ghazālī (d.1111 CE), who advocated for creation *ex nihilo*. al-Ghazālī's most fundamental challenge was that these two philosophers had allowed the Neoplatonic structure to become a primary discourse over what philosophical doctrines they thought were justified by the Qur'an itself. In addition, he thought that their position seemed to imply the eternity of the world (as, like Plotinus, it was a necessary emanation of God) and that what appeared to be temporal things were uncreated. Aquinas appropriated many of al-Ghazālī's insights into his own reasoning about the relationship between God and creation, as well as faith and reason.

2.4 Pantheism and Panentheism

Maybe it is a question of focus or changing the emphasis? So, where the concerns of monotheism are not in view, the notion of creation as a divine act is less prominent or distinct. Take, for example, a view that has affinities with an emanationist one, pantheism. This is the monistic notion that God and the world are the same thing – a view commonly associated with eastern traditions like Hinduism or Taoism. In this case, speaking about 'God' and 'creation' becomes tautologous. This creates problems with definitions. It was Schopenhauer who argued that pantheism presented a conceptual confusion that effectively adds nothing to our understanding of either God or creation, for 'to call the world God is not to explain it; it is only to enrich our language with a superfluous synonym for the word world' (Schopenhauer 1974, 99). Michael Levine replies that Schopenhauer's protest misses its mark because it assumes what pantheism actually denies: theism (see Levine 1994, 26–32). Of course, if one distinguishes God from the world *as a theist does*, then making them synonymous will seem like a dissipation of the theistic concept of divinity. However, Levine claims that another concept, 'Unity', is at play in pantheism: 'For the pantheist, God and the world are generally not and should not be taken as intentionally equivalent. Something about the world, namely, the fact that it is taken to be an all-inclusive divine Unity – is the reason for calling the world "God"' (28). This, for Levine, has implications for the idea of creation. So, if the storyline of theism (from the 'beginning to the end') makes creation a crucial element, 'pantheism rejects the theistic storyline.' A pantheist may, in fact, regard existence to be a brute fact, and therefore what is important is not origins but the existence of a divine Unity which pantheists 'need not interpret . . . as itself necessary or ultimately explicable.' In which case, pantheism does not require a doctrine of creation (179–80).

There may be many reasons to advocate for a more pantheistic view that stems from traditional scriptural or cultural sources, or from a philosophical vision about the unity of selves in an eternal monism. This will certainly be the emphasis within Indian traditions. However, as we have indicated, it is not only difficult but perhaps even a category error to attempt to compare the pantheistic conception of Unity with creation as a divinely initiated event, or in terms of a *relationship* between creation and transcendence. Nevertheless, there are other pantheistic types of thinking that are more consistent with the idea of divine creation. One is panentheism ('all-in-God'). Although some have argued that the varieties of panentheism mean that it is unstable as a concept,[10] there are some basic principles that seem to be shared. So, fundamentally, 'panentheism is the view that all is contained within the divine, although God is also more than the world' (Clayton 2011, 365). As some conception of the divine indwelling of creation is present in both, panentheism offers the promise of a bridge between Indian and Western traditions.[11] Nevertheless, perhaps one difference is that, unlike the impersonal ultimate of *Vedāntic* traditions, Christian panentheists want to retain the idea of a personal God who is beyond creation. At the same time, they reject the stronger description of creation as being *other* than God that one would associate with the creation *ex nihilo* model. This means that panentheism is criticized by both pantheists – who see an unnecessary separation of God from the world – and supporters of the classical *ex nihilo* stance, who criticize panentheists for over-complicating a clear distinction between God and creation. With panentheism, although God's *essence* is unchanged, the world's experience is also God's experience, thus 'real change occurs not in the divine nature but in the divine experience' (Clayton 2011, 365). This is something that Mikael Stenmark describes as 'ontological inclusion' (Stenmark 2019, 27). Although God stands above the world, the world is somehow included as a part of the divine story and its completion.

Some modern supporters of panentheism see it as the most satisfactory creational model for harmonizing with evolutionary science (see Brierley

---

[10] See Gregerson 2004.
[11] For example, Keith Ward traces a connection along one strand of panentheism (what might be called 'expressivist') between Ramanuja (c.1017–1137 CE) and that of the German idealist philosopher Hegel (1770–1831). See Ward 2004.

2004, 13). In this connection, one of the powerful philosophical influences historically for this way of conceiving the divine ontology is the German idealist philosopher, Georg Wilhelm Friedrich Hegel (1770–1831). In Hegel's system, God is not only Absolute Geist, but also that which is the culmination of the unfolding historical process instigated by its action to achieve a final, complete consciousness and self-awareness, which binds its own ultimate reality together *with the process of becoming*. Hegel thinks it is false to set the infinite in opposition to the finite (or God 'above' or 'apart' from the world). In fact, for something to be properly infinite, he thinks it must include everything within itself, including the *finite*. In which case, the world must somehow be contained in God. As we said, what makes Hegel's philosophy so appealing is its apparent resonance with the evolutionary description of natural and human development. God is a dynamic reality that is ever evolving and growing. However, perhaps this is the very feature that makes it unappealing for many as well. That is, for many believers, God is perceived as a secure foundation in the midst of change rather than *being* change ('I am the same yesterday, today, and forever' Heb.13.8). Thus, Keith Ward suggests that at the root of the dispute there are different understandings of perfection. Whereas in Aquinas' view, perfection is something that is changeless and unbounded, the Hegelian panentheist ideal includes change and relationships (Ward 2004, 65–66).

Nevertheless, there is perhaps a difference between describing panentheism in present or in eschatological terms. For example, in Colossians 1:17 it says, 'and he is before all things, and in him all things hold together'. This appears to be an ontological statement about the nature of created reality *now* and would seem to support a panentheistic stance. However, does this mean that we are obliged to conclude that the evil and malice that are part of creation's present reality are also *held together* by God? Such an interpretation would seem to be refuted by passages like 1 John 1.5, which says, 'God is light; in him is no darkness at all.' Thus, should panentheism be properly applied to an *eschatological* context, which refers to a future hope when evil and suffering are ended and there is a final consummation: 'On that day you will realize that I am in my Father, and you are in me, and I am in you' (John 14.20)?

Another argument by advocates of panentheism concerns its alleged moral appeal, particularly for process thinkers. That is, a premium is placed on the attractiveness of 'relationality', or the sense of divine dialogue and mutual interaction with creation. For example, Phillip Clayton says that the 'process insight— that a responsive God is greater, is more fully God, than a dispassionate God-above history – beautifully summarizes a deep underlying motivation of panentheism' (Clayton 2001, 215). Here, the issue becomes one about how a particular creational picture makes God look more or less attractive, morally speaking, as a proposition. Is the panentheist's God – who is above creation but also includes creation ontologically – more appealing? Or, returning to our earlier discussion, is the complete Unity of God and creation in pantheism a more satisfying account of existence and experience?

Some might be repelled by the metaphysics of pantheism or panentheism. For example, the French philosopher Maurice Merleau-Ponty abhorred the idea that creation has been absorbed by the transcendent or is made valuable only by connecting it to a higher authority than itself. He writes that Judeo-Christian thinking is 'haunted by the threat of acosmism' and he wants to retain the wonder of the world *for itself*, without reference to God. Thus, our wonder before the world is not to be obtained by moving 'toward the unity of consciousness as the foundation of the world; rather it steps back in order to see transcendences spring forth ... ' (Merleau-Ponty 2012 [1945], lxxvii). That is, Merleau-Ponty wants to set the world free from the transcendent in order for it to shine on its own terms. Ostensibly, this view might appear only attractive to an atheist, but perhaps it also underscores the importance of the freedom of creation that can only be afforded by creational models that *separate* God from the world and allow creation itself to be very good? We shall return to this shortly.

A variation on this theme is the problem of distinguishing finite and infinite categories. So, one important question is whether pantheism or panentheism allows us to say anything meaningful about finite existence? This may be less acute in the latter than the former, but there seems to be little room for doing justice to finite substances. So, Austin Farrer suggests that a pantheist in particular faces a dilemma about how to speak discretely about finite substances and the divine. For example, would speaking about the world as a kind of 'god' depend on us asserting the '*illusion* of finite substance', and would not this be tantamount to a perceptual error on our part? If we grant that finite substances are not illusory and have their own independence, so to speak, then we are compelled to adopt a more standard metaphysical ordering that separates finite from infinite (see Farrer 1959, 20).

2.5 God and Creation: Expressing the Difference

Alongside the matter of the total freedom of God to create is the question of how we might describe God as being *different* from creation. If emanationist views tend to imply a spiritual and material hierarchy, they ultimately fail to grant creation itself any true independence from the divine. Claiming that God is totally free to create, or that creation is an unnecessary free act that adds nothing to God, gives us some indication of the proper nature of this relationship.

Basically, it suggests that the link between God and creation is not necessary or required. Let us unpack this. So, with Plotinus' emanationism, it is not apparent how this difference is to be expressed, except perhaps by increments or gradations; nor is it altogether clear from his writings that he was consistent in his statements about God and the world. This is something that Kathryn Tanner draws our attention to. So, as we have said, Plotinus presents a 'serially proceeding chain of being' that appears to place the divine within a spectrum that is involved in the world (see Tanner 1988, 42–44). However, in other passages, he would seem to be arguing for the simplicity of God. Especially when he describes the 'One' as 'the unitary, simple and undifferentiated ground of all mind and being.' This would make the One something that is transcategorial and cannot be understood in terms of the kinds of binary oppositions or causal necessities as instantiated within creation itself. Ironically, we see the claim 'God is simple' being made in the theologies of non-emanationist figures like Irenaeus, Augustine, Aquinas, or al-Ghazālī.

To say that God is simple is not a pejorative reference and is not intended to make God inferior in some respect, rather, it is linked to God's categorical uniqueness. So, if we return to Irenaeus, he seeks to make clear that comparing God's action (for example, the flow between mind and thought and word) with human experience leads to error:

> They [heretics] apply to the Father of all things, who, they assert, is unknown to all, the actions that occur in men and women lead to the spoken word [...] For the Father is far removed from the actions and passions that men and women experience. He is simple and not composite; with all members of similar nature, being entirely similar and equal to himself (Irenaeus 2012, 43).

Describing God as simple is a way of distinguishing God from *all things*. Augustine (354–430 CE) gives us the following definition: 'There is then one sole Good, which is simple, and therefore unchangeable, and that is God. By this good all good things were created, but they are not simple, and for that reason they are changeable' (Augustine 2003, 440). Then he proceeds to explain:

> The reason why a nature is called simple is that it cannot lose any attribute it possesses, that there is no difference between what it is and what it has, as there is, for example, between a vessel and the liquid it contains, a body and its colour, the atmosphere and its light or heat, the soul and its wisdom. None of these *is* what it contains' (441).

We can understand this if we make a contrast with creatures (See Oliver 2017, 44). Creatures are not simple but composites of many parts. Take a human person.

We can point to their bodily features, their characteristics (e.g., moral), and their particular attributes or talents. But, these aspects can come and go – my body may be changed by an accident, my character may evolve for the better or worse, my talents may diminish, and if I have authority, I may lose it. Of course, I still exist, and so these other aspects are 'additions' to my existence; but the basic point is that a human being's existence plus their accidental qualities make up the kind of thing that *human creatures* are. We are comprised structurally as a 'what-it-is-and-what-it-has' thing. So, in contrast, to say God is simple is to assert that God is not a composite like creatures, what God is (God's existence) and what God has (God's attributes, character, etc.) are the same. Perhaps a more familiar way of stating this is that 'love' is not something that is added to God, rather God *is* love. Saying God's existence and God's attributes are the same thing means that God does not change as we change – God does not become more or less wise; does not lose the capacity to love; does not grow or diminish in knowledge or power – God simply *is these things*.

Going further, we might also say that 'God is simple' is a formal way of properly referring to the divine. Burrell, following Thomas Aquinas, argues that 'God's simpleness and God's eternity are part of what assures us we are talking about divinity' (Burrell 2004, 6). So, Aquinas describes God as the 'beginning and end of all things' who 'has whatever must belong to the first cause of all things which is beyond all that is caused' (Burrell 1979, 14).[12] He advances a method of understanding God that proceeds on the basis of negation. Thus, 'the ways in which God does not exist will become apparent if we rule out from him everything inappropriate, such as compositeness, change and the like' (14). Again, this is a 'logic appropriate to the discourse about God' (17). Thus, in order to be the source of creation God has to be formally distinct from it. Only a simple God can 'produce being absolutely', and for Aquinas 'creation is the proper act of God alone' (Levering 2017, 107).

These are perhaps the products of a high scholasticism in philosophy, and modern philosophical accounts present other models, but this is not to say that such reasoning has no application. How does such formal logic of God's simplicity and eternity function in religious life? Going back to the mother in 2 Macc.7.28, we see that it is part of a confession about God's total supremacy in terms of power and the ability to provide. Ian McFarland (reflecting on Theophilus of Antioch) puts it this way: 'If God is to be confessed as Lord without qualification, then everything that is not God must depend on God for its existence without qualification' (McFarland 2014, 2). The logical categorization of God as the 'beginning and end of all things' is the basis for confessing

---

[12] Citing *Summa*, 1.12.12.

that God utterly transcends our existence: '"For my thoughts are not your thoughts, neither are your ways my ways," declares the Lord. "As the heavens are higher than the earth, so are my ways higher than your ways and my thoughts than your thoughts"' (Is 55.8–9). The Danish philosopher, Soren Kierkegaard, gave existential expression to this when he said that 'there is an infinite, radical, qualitative difference between God and man' (Kierkegaard 2012, 687). This was not intended to be an obscurantist remark; on the contrary, he thought that it was the basis for a subjective 'passion of the infinite' (Kierkegaard 1992, 181).

However, if we establish such an infinite abyss between God and creation, what does this make of the language we use about God and about the attributes we ascribe? If God is simple, not a composite, then we cannot apply 'properties' to God in a way that is univocal with our own. Although he did not develop this in a systematic way, Aquinas' solution is to speak of analogical predication. We cannot speak of God univocally (using words with identical meanings – e.g., 'father'), nor is our language wholly equivocal (radically different). However, the reason why we ought not to conclude that God is linguistically out of reach is that, if we recall, Aquinas thought of creation as something fundamental to understanding our being. Being as *creatura*. Thus, there is an affinity between creator and created, and this allows us to think of our language about God as *analogous*. Reality for Aquinas is not just a product of a neutral rationality; instead, reality – as divinely created – possesses a kind of luminosity. That is, 'the reality of things is itself their light' (Aquinas 1996, 61).

Again, taking this thought, we could go further and ask about the expression of 'analogy' in religious life and the ways in which this connects the creator with the created. Perhaps one way of thinking about this is through the concept of glory. For instance, Kelsey finds God's glory in the 'peculiar way in which God creatively relates to reality other than himself' (Kelsey 2009, 316). What can he mean? That somehow the peculiarity of God's engagement with the world is *glorious*? So, when Aquinas speaks of being as *creatura*, and reality as a 'light', perhaps there is relationship being described between creation and the creator that is doxological: 'The heavens declare the glory of God; the skies proclaim the work of his hands' (Ps 19.1) Though there is an eschatological dimension to glory as that *which is yet to come* it also speaks of a reality that is already present in creation now. For the Italian political philosopher, Giorgio Agamben, glory is a theological strategy that is used to cover over the complexities of theological distinctions. He writes: 'Glory is the place where theology attempts to think the difficult conciliation between immanent trinity and economic trinity, *theologia* and *oikonomia*, being and praxis, God in himself and God for us' (Agamben 2011, 208). Setting aside Agamben's idiosyncratic use of glory in his political thinking, this might be another way of describing the mysterious relationship between creation and God and how it is expressed *in creation*. Aquinas, speaking philosophically, uses analogy to bridge the logical chasm, but perhaps 'glory' is something that vividly exhibits the incomprehensible experience of gratuity and shows by its light the mystery of God in relation to creation.

And yet, some might still be thinking of the difference between the divine and the world in terms of straightforward oppositions. However, what is being said by thinkers like Aquinas is that this relationship is not to be thought of as symmetrical. That is, God's relation to the world is wholly other and not a contrasting expression of oppositions (light and dark, spirit and matter, up and down). Moreover, God does not simply function as the *explanation* for existence either, which would, in effect, draw God into a causal and hierarchical network of explanations. This latter point is subtle, but it is one of the reasons why Aquinas did not think of creation *ex nihilo* necessarily in terms of beginnings or explanations, indeed, it would logically be compatible with an eternal universe because Aquinas thinks that creation *ex nihilo* is primarily an account of the *proper relation* between God and the universe. So, although there is little controversy surrounding the idea of creation as something that has taken place in the past from the human perspective of history, the meaning of *creatio ex nihilo* concerns a far more profound relationship between the Creator and the creation. As Aquinas argued, creation cannot be described in terms of a movement or change in the divine; instead, it describes a relationship: 'the very dependence of created being on the principle whereby it is produced' (Aquinas 1923a, 27).

The crucial point is that, because of what Kierkegaard called the infinite qualitative distinction between God and the created order, the language of symmetrical difference or calculable distance breaks down. In this sense, God's simplicity and absolute relational difference from creation allows paradoxically for a profound intimacy. It should be clear, then, that this is a difference of an entirely different order from that of basic oppositions, in the words of Kathryn Tanner, 'divine transcendence exceeds all oppositional contrasts characteristic of relations among finite beings' (Tanner 1988, 56). The term that Tanner (and Burrell) uses for this difference is *non-contrastive*. Put simply, as we have said, we cannot use the language of contrasts to describe the difference between God and creation. One of the most oft-cited accounts of this is supplied by Robert Sokolowski in *The God of Faith and Reason* (1982), who uses the phrase 'Christian distinction' to refer to it. Burrell seeks to extend this beyond the Christian reference and also finds similar distinctions expressed in both Judaism and Islam, particularly the thought of Maimonides and al-Ghazālī. For Sokolowski, this 'distinction' reinforces a sense of divine mystery that, because it resists rational formulation, allows us to hold together seeming contradictions as mysteries apprehended by faith. Critics might see this as an intellectual white flag – the appeal to mystery. However, the point of the last few pages has been to outline the philosophical logic that seeks to speak of that which is 'the beginning and end of all things' or the exceedingly transcendent nature of the creator God. There is, therefore, a paradoxical consistency here. The non-contrastive distinction creates a space for mystery, or perhaps it opens into a realm where only the mention of *glory* would appear to suffice.

2.6 Intimacy and Distance

Nevertheless, does this accentuate the distance between God and creation? As we said earlier, one of the attractive aspects of the emanationist view is that it makes the link between the world and God appear, at first sight, closer and more intimate than with the *creatio ex nihilo* view. This is also the case with the broader pantheist position, which identifies God with the cosmos. For the purposes of building a close connection between God and World, both the emanationist (though in an incremental sense) and pantheist view seems admirably well-suited. Contrary to the seeming dualism of creation by a God *outside* of the world, these more monist viewpoints appear to suggest a deep unity simply by asserting a basic ontology of God present within and through all that exists. Figures like Sallie McFague, who prefers the more organic portrayal of the world as God's body, are seeking to rebel against the seeming hierarchical picture of a dominating, supreme God outside the action who subdues creation to the divine will. Their objections to the classical models of the likes of Augustine and Aquinas are more of the moral than logical kind. In fact, it is the kind of logical approach that such writers accuse of alienating God from creation or allegedly installing a power structure that seems opposed to solidarity and intimacy. Thus, ostensibly, God's close intimacy with creation is affirmed by a more pantheistic embodied model.

However, can it be described as close or intimate at all if a sense of otherness is actually removed? That is, unlike theism pantheistic models do not place the emphasis on a relationship between God and the world. For example, Levine suggests that pantheistic goals tend to be described in terms of a state rather than a personal relation. An individual 'state' results, through meditation and contemplation, from 'an understanding of, and right relation to, the Unity.' Levine is not altogether clear about what the ontology of this Unity might be because the state of our relationship to it is 'partly dependent upon other people and things, the state the pantheist seeks is not something achievable in isolation.'

Although pantheists do not create the Unity, claims Levine, they can 'contribute to it' (Levine 1994, 346, 348). Whereas this appears to conjure a collaborative metaphysical picture, we should be sceptical about considering it as a genuine model of a possible relationship between creator and creation, which would be essentially a theistic imposition onto the pantheist's ontology.

However, it would be untrue to say that there can be no resonances at all with theistic ideas here, and certainly more panentheist or process theologies will be able to find common interests. But if this might be conceived as the more harmonious model of the *relationship* of the divine to the creation, or for human-to-human relations, it seems to come with the price tag of a loss of otherness. That is, pantheistic models are not really about closeness in terms of a relation, rather, they appear to advocate for full immersion and absorption of identity. We might say that all creatures are equally contained or absorbed in divinity, but it is not clear if the term 'equality' is apposite in this conception because there is no relational dynamic or otherness in view—all is divine.

So, perhaps we need to be more specific and speak about what Janice McRandal has called the 'closeness of transcendence' (see McRandal 2015,40–44). Although it might seem counterintuitive to talk about creation *ex nihilo* as asserting anything other than radical difference, when understood as a non-contrastive difference, as we discussed earlier, it implies something surprising. For Irenaeus, the effect of the non-contrastive distinction is that it confounds the language of opposites: light and dark, presence and absence, God and humanity, eternal perfection and worldly instability. Or rather, such opposites are not part of the same order of reality, and so God does not stand at a calculable distance, like at the end of a great chain of existence, from creation. This would appear to greatly magnify the distance of God from the creation, however, the reverse is the case. So, if closeness with God is sought then asserting God's utter freedom through a non-contrastive relationship means that rather than relating to the world as, say, an upper storey relates to a lower storey, or through a sequential emanationist procession, or through some kind of divine infusion into the world with its limitations of space and time, God 'may be related in the same direct fashion to every link in the chain, as the productive agent for the whole' (Tanner 1988, 44). That is to say, the non-contrastive view suggests that there is a radical sovereign freedom in terms of God's relation to the creation. Here is another, perhaps more radical, notion of intimacy that arises out of a non-contrastive model of the divine/creation relationship. B Richard Norris explains Irenaeus' view:

> God is the measureless context of all being, as well as its source: different from any creature, but separated from none [...] nothing sets a limit to

[God's] power and presence. What makes God *different* from every creature – his eternal and ingenerate simplicity – is thus, for Irenaeus, precisely what assures his direct and intimate *relation* with every creature (Norris 1966, 70).

Additionally, if we set aside the idea of origins from the root meaning, then it becomes possible to talk of *creatio ex nihilo* 'in the present tense' (Jenson 2004, 19). Alan Torrance argues that it is vitally important to underscore this point because if the idea of creation is consigned to the past, so to speak, then it cannot play a role in our understanding of the present and our lived existence in this world now. So, we ought to see creation as somehow related *immediately* to the whole of existence. This perspective says something about the sheer giftedness of every moment and action: 'we are now obliged to interpret every aspect of spatio-temporal existence and every kind of particular existent, be it an object, or a process, or a law, or any form of connectedness between events, in all their spatio-temporal particularity, as requiring to be understood as created *ex nihilo*' (Torrance 2004, 102).

This also suggests that all created beings and things are *equally* near (or far) from the divine. This emerges both from a consideration of the non-contrastive distinction that we have discussed and from creation's freedom. Colin Gunton expresses a fine (but important) distinction between a Neoplatonic emanationist sense and a biblical sense: 'It is noticeable that in the Genesis account God does not say "Be", but "let there be". In a similar vein, Burrell makes a point about 'created freedom being proper to creatures' (Burrell 2004, 6). Thus, what characterizes the nature of being creatures in relation to monotheism? There is a greater stress on what we might call the giving of space to be to a reality that is other than God' (Gunton 2002, 5). Matter does not exist along a hierarchical spectrum —stretching back to an eternal, recalcitrant chaos that was (and is) being subdued by God. Ian McFarland explains:

> the implications of creation from nothing are not consistent with the kind of hierarchical vision of the created order that would justify narrow focus on the church, or even on humanity considered more broadly. Most importantly, where all creatures are equally dependent on God for their existence, there can be no sense in which any creature is ontologically closer to God than any other: the most unimpressive lump of rock is no more distant from God than the most glorious of the seraphim (McFarland 2014, 185).

So, to be creatures is to acknowledge that they are 'not God' and therefore no one is closer or more removed from God. Once again, there are important interpersonal dynamics that arise out of such circumstances. It is not only the ontological fact of createdness that is equally shared by all, it is also that a wholehearted participation in creation means that we are compelled to affirm our own finitude and particularity. Another way of expressing this would be to say that our creational experience does not invite us to imagine that our own particularity should be universalized. In so doing, a genuine creation spirituality does not presume to acquire a vision of creation's *totality* but becomes one that affirms our own particularity and exhorts us to recognize that others inhabit their own particularity as a condition of their creaturehood (See Wilson 2013, 23–26).

Again, this takes us back to our opening questions, where we asked about creation as a religious concern. Is the limitation of creaturely reality something to be shunned in favour of more transcendent goals? Does an affection for the finitude of created existence bring us too close to corruptibility and the distractions of the senses? Perhaps these are rather Greek prejudices – keen to prefer the mode of archetypes. However, the point is that when we enter creation's horizon, we find *creaturehood*.

2.7 Challenges to *ex nihilo*

Although *creatio ex nihilo* represents the most widely accepted explanation in theistic thinking, it has been subjected to major challenges. Common critiques centre on questions of power, hierarchy, and the problem of evil and suffering. For example, the feminist theologian, Sallie McFague, thinks that *creatio ex nihilo* is a 'dangerous notion' with its seeming monarchical picture that 'God created hierarchically, with the physical subordinated to the spiritual ...' (McFague 1997, 109). Alluding to the influence of Gordon Kaufman, she complains that the relationship between God and World according to the *ex nihilo* model is an assymetrical one and 'God and world are only distantly related ... ' She recoils at the idea of a supreme God who rules the universe and where all the power 'is on God's side;' something which she takes to imply that 'God can only be God if we are nothing' (64). The reasons why McFague thinks that the connection between God's power and egotistical monarchical intentions is self-evident are not made wholly clear, but it perhaps reflects her preference for a different picture of God that she articulates as 'open, caring, inclusive, interdependent, changing, mutual and creative' (14). McFague's eco-feminist creation-spirituality rightly concentrates on other important creational themes that are borne out of nurturing models of God as mother, lover, and friend, and the overall spiritual vision is one that seeks to overcome the disconnect between humanity and the natural world. She makes important criticisms that lean towards a more evolutionary, developmental portrayal of creation that seeks to avoid a top-down relation.

However, the critique of the dualism between God and world thrives on (and overplays) the contrastive oppositions between divine and human, power and weakness, spirit and matter, that the non-contrastive view makes redundant. Moreover, the alleged distance of the God-World relation in the classical model is something that McFague critiques using metaphorical rhetoric that plays heavily on parental imagery. This is consistent with an overall theological method that she advocates – a metaphorical theology which has as its primary task a demythologization of life using 'poetic, imagistic' tools and which recommends 'identifying and elucidating primary metaphors and models from contemporary experience' (32). However, if this is the principal method, then there should presumably be few embargoes on which metaphors we choose to characterize the meaning of distance. On the question of distance between God and creation, McFague conjures an image of regal indifference, but might distance be dressed in other guises? For example, take David Bentley Hart's description of the distance required for the beauty of creation to be admired:

> If the realm of created difference has its being for God's pleasure (Rev 4.11), then the distance of creation from God and every distance within creation belong originally to an interval of appraisal and approbation, the distance of delight. God's pleasure – the beauty creation possesses in this regard – underlies the distinct being of creation, and so beauty is the first and truest word concerning all that appears within being, beauty is the showing of what is; God looked upon what he had wrought and saw that it was good (Hart 2003, 18).

This is not necessarily to dismiss McFague's reading of the alleged distance from God and creation in the classical tradition, but it might indicate that if we are licensed to think in terms of metaphor, then this is another account – not the distance of domination or subjugation but of a lover's delight.

However, continuing with critiques based on power, in her influential text, *Face of the Deep* (2003), Catherine Keller wishes to distance creation theology from what she labels the 'triumphant *logos*' of the early Church Fathers (Keller 2003, 64). Keller is captivated by the 'deeps' over which the Spirit hovers in Gen. 1.2. In her own words, she advocates for a 'tehomophilic' account of God and creation as opposed to a 'tehomophobic' interpretation where the creator seeks to 'erase the chaos of creation' (xix). Similar to McFague, chief amongst her criticisms is the perceived rhetoric of sheer power with a God that 'needs nothing but his own logos to create' (53). Drawing on the statement in Gen 1.2, she believes that the potential of *tehom* (primordial deep) has been repressed or dispossessed of its involvement in creation by what she interprets as a domineering masculine model. Rather than set up an opposition of creation versus chaos, the novelty of Keller's approach is to be found in the way in which she seeks to embrace 'chaos' or the *tehom* in positive terms and how she interprets the tehomic depths as possessive of creational vitality.[13] Moreover, in contrast with the logos of *ex nihilo,* which she claims drives creation in a linear movement forward towards its triumphant conclusion, she thinks that her tehomic vision gives rise to 'a helical, recapitulatory sense of history' (Keller 2003, 56). Overriding the 'monotone of transcendence', God 'lures self-organizing systems out of fluctuating possibilities' (195).

Keller outlines vividly her objection to the organizing effect of the Logos when viewed through a Hellenistic lens, which she claims calcifies paradoxes into the 'unquestionabilities' of Nicene Christology. She laments this historical development in early Church thinking, which she argues hardens theological fluidity and makes 'interdimensional oscillations of a more mobile incarnation freeze'. These criticisms emerge from a sense that the free, intrinsic value of creation in all its chaotic diversity has been stultified by the 'timeless logos' (58). If not the 'triumphant logos' that underpins creation theology, then what does Keller propose instead? She wants us to overcome the 'tehomophobia' of *creatio ex nihilo* and put chaos to work. The *tehom* is the place of becoming, the world is formed 'out of a chaotic something', it is a *creatio cooperationis*: 'non-linear interactions between Elohim and Tehom' (117).

Some critics of Keller's version of creation tend to find a weakness in what Keller herself takes to be a virtue, namely that chaos is allowed to merge with the divine (Elohim and Tehom) as part of the creation's formation. Although her overall picture may be interpreted as just another version of pantheism, her use of chaos is particularly idiosyncratic. In spite of her romantic positive vision, chaos itself is more commonly associated (in the ancient world, generally not just the 'logocentric' early Church) with the dismantling of order and harmony rather than a positive movement or growth in creation. This is a point made by Eric Vail who suggests that Keller could have simply chosen another term, like *profundus*, rather than chaos (Vail 2012, 180). However, in the end, is it just a matter of nomenclature, or is Keller proposing something that should be considered a creation model at all? That is, rather than supplying an alternative version of creation, her fixation on the constant motion of the deep and the 'rhythmic life of all creatures' (Keller 2003, 238) seems to have little room for the discrete actions of a creator God.

In seeking to reinstate creation *ex nihilo*, Rowan Williams has this idea of the monarchical God in his sights when he argues that the picture of the subjugation of creation is founded upon some basic misconceptions. Much of this relates to

---

[13] For a discussion of the place of chaos in creation, see Vail 2012. Vail discusses Keller's work in chap.5.

what we discussed earlier about the non-contrastive relationship of God to creation. So, God does not dominate or subdue a primordial chaos and creation is not an imposition of the divine will onto something pre-existing: 'With God alone, I am dealing with what does not need to construct or negotiate an identity, what is free to be itself without the process of struggle' (Williams 1999, 72–73). If God is wholly free to create unnecessarily, then there is no 'triumphant logos' as such because there is nothing that has been triumphed over in terms of a contest. This makes the opening statement in Genesis that heralds the creation, 'let there be', sound less like an act of power and authority and more like a stepping aside that allows the other to exist and flourish. So, there is an important clarification concerning the relationship between God's will and our own natures. God creates in freedom and affirms createdness in itself. Again:

> God does not impose pre-ordained extra-human roles rather than the ones we naturally inhabit. In short, creaturehood is *intended*, it is not the victim of an exterior force that needs to be overcome or exceeded. Creation spirituality becomes problematic if it is a project to *overcome* our 'nature' or a flight away from creaturehood (69).[14]

We shall consider creaturehood further in our next section, but even if we accept that the relationship between God and creation does not have to be interpreted in terms of dominance and power, there still remains the insistent question about the kind of creation we experience and the seeming ubiquity of evil and suffering. It is all very well speaking about the beauties of a creation that is 'let-be', but does the idea of God creating in absolute freedom face an insuperable moral difficulty when confronted with the horrors of the world? In which case, is a more incarnational or embodied model of creation more appropriate after all; or one that conceives a God who evinces solidarity in the midst of things? The problem of evil is one of the chief reasons why some theologians have questioned the classical model and sought to consider a different conception of the divine using process thought.

A prominent representative, David Griffin, says: 'the problem of evil is a problem for those theistic positions that hold the doctrine of omnipotence implied by the doctrine of creation out of nothing' (Griffin 1981, 104). We saw earlier that David Bentley Hart's view was not to abandon creation *ex nihilo* – which he saw as being essential for the very definition of divinity – but instead to resolve the question of evil with a final consummation that includes salvation for all. That is, he sought not to exacerbate the problem with the 'infernalist' addendum of hell. No loose ends – all shall be well. But the process view of

---

[14] See chap. 5 of Williams (1999) for a discussion of McFague. Further, see Williams 2016, chap. 4.

Griffin and others seeks to deal with the issue of suffering by rethinking the meaning of God. In fact, Griffin is unabashed in affirming the model of God working to subdue a primordial chaos that we associated with the Greek ideas earlier as well as with Catherine Keller's work a moment ago.

Underlying the process view is the work of Alfred North Whitehead, who argued in his seminal work *Process and Reality* that God is not exceptional but rather the 'chief exemplification' of 'metaphysical principles' (Whitehead 1978, 343). There is also an aversion expressed by writers such as Norman Pittenger and David Griffin about the idea of God intervening in an occasionalist show of omnipotence that seems scarce most of the time. The objections will resonate very much with the contemporary postmodern zeitgeist that speaks against the notion of 'power' imposing itself and overruling the identity of the other. Thus, in the process view, God does not act in sovereign power, but instead persuades and coerces, urging the world through the 'lure of love' (Pittenger) to use its agency towards overcoming evil.

Jon Levenson makes the same kind of appeal as do process theologians (and Keller). We are not entitled to be optimistic about the outcome of the 'malign process', and he offers no decisive vision of God's victory. In fact, he thinks that the biblical accounts tell a story of the survival of 'chaos' after the initial victory of God at the beginning, the days of Noah being one such example, where the state of the world was a cause of divine regret. God may have covenanted not to destroy the world again by water, but God's ordering of the world is 'irresistable, but not constant or inevitable' (Levenson 1994, 14). Thus, on the one hand, his theology of creation concerns the way in which God is being 'triumphant over all rivals' (47), but any confidence in this outcome is undermined by Levenson's attraction to the drama of history that exhibits the 'enormity of the risk' in bringing about an eventual 'life sustaining order' (156). Here we see writ large a difference in priority. For example, whereas Janet Soskice speaks of creation as something *about God* rather than the cosmos, for Levenson it is about the 'grandeur of faith' shown by a cultic people in the face of the persistence of evil (147).

However, is there too great a preponderance of the power of the *story*? A noble conception of solidarity: a divine creator working in the mix with creatures towards a good outcome sounds supremely empathetic, but is it ontologically adequate? So, the question remains whether we can genuinely see process theology as advancing anything like the traditional monotheistic all-powerful picture that we find in the Abrahamic traditions and, therefore, whether there is any support for it beyond a small revisionist constituency? Despite its seeming solidarity with human experience and suffering, in the end, its comforting platitudes scarcely conceal the powerless god that is struggling to succeed. John Hick described it as 'metaphysically unsatisfying', and Joanna Leidenhag provides a neat summary of its problems:

> The only comfort that process theology provides, in light of such metaphysical necessity, is that God (necessarily) suffers too. This is the Consequent Nature of God, where all experiences of th world are received into God and inform the ongoing lure of God. Thus, the suffering of actual occasions is not lost, nor is it meaningless. However, it does seem hopeless. Process theology provides no guarantee that God's desire for good will have victory over evil (Leidenhag 2021, 121).

3 Createdness

Some of the pictures of divine creation in the previous section, such as the emanationist, pantheist, or panentheistic, or those accounts that present God as one who creates not *ex nihilo* but from a primordial chaos or the depths (*creatio ex profundis*), affirm a unity (or even identity) between the divine and the human world. These pictures vaunt a special intimacy or relationality, but in such cases, one is also left wondering what integrity remains for human creativity and self-determination, or if there can be a created order that exists in and for itself. This is perhaps one area where the *ex nihilo* picture shows its strength. The freedom of God to create unnecessarily serves to release humanity from the burden of shouldering the divine project, simply because God does not require the world to partner in some mutual exchange to realize any further perfection in God. Creation does not reflect any lack in God, our own existence is not helping God to *become a better God*.

This is a view that is expressed by several scholars, such as Rowan Williams or Edward Schillebeeckx, and its virtue is that it liberates us to be what we are: created (see Williams 1999, 72–73). Finitude is not to be regarded with regret. To be creatures is to have been given an identity that is precisely not God; nor is it *faded* being in respect of its relationship to some distant bright reality at the other end of the chain; it is a gifted being that is other than God. This is central to a presentation of creation as something to be embraced and which is contrasted with more gnostic conceptions where there is a spiritual world which is preferred above this one, or even pantheistic views of creation where the world is not distinguished but is regarded as a part of the divine unity. For Schillebeeckx, like Williams, the problem with these other conceptions is that they imply that the betterment of man [sic] 'logically consists in raising himself above his human condition and the circumstances of his world and his own particular specific human character in order to attain to a *more-than-creaturely* status' (113). However, we should clarify that to affirm the creaturely life is not the same as advocating for immanent interpretations of transcendence. Of course, much debate has taken place in the literature regarding *immanence* and the discussion on the relationship between the transcendent and immanent is well rehearsed across many traditions. This kind of discussion can end up becoming a reductionist project where one favours immanence over transcendence or translates transcendence into immanence. A radical example of this is the reductionist work of Ludwig Feuerbach (1804–72), who argued that the objects of theology were essentially anthropological ones in disguise. Instead, reflection on the created life relates to the goals of the quotidian level that we have already mentioned, as well as the visibility of the 'penultimate'. The ontological conception being deployed is the idea of created life as sheer 'gift', and this affirmation challenges us to specify the purpose of human activity and the kinds of work that humanity can do meaningfully in that context.

Perhaps one of the most influential thinkers to draw attention to the importance of the everyday in religious life was the 20th C theologian Dietrich Bonhoeffer. In his work *Creation and Fall*, he says that God addresses us as follows: 'You are a free creature, so now be that. You are free, so be free, you are a creature, so be a creature' (Bonhoeffer 1997, 85). There is something powerful about how we are *addressed* by God and how this determines what humans are commissioned to accomplish. Although this is not a summons towards a 'banal this-worldliness', Bonhoeffer thinks that it nonetheless involves living 'unreservedly in life's duties, problems, successes and failures, experiences and perplexities.' The world can develop its own music, so to speak, with God as the *cantus firmus*. Bonhoeffer wishes to claim 'the whole of *earthly* life for God.' In doing so, he turns our attention to the 'penultimate' and he uses this concept to break down the barriers between the Christian and the secular world. He thinks it is of profound importance to translate religion into something that makes sense to ordinary people: 'What do a church, a community, a sermon, a liturgy, a Christian life mean in a religionless world? How do we speak of God – without religion, that is, without the temporally conditioned presuppositions of metaphysics, inwardness, and so on? How do we speak in a secular way about God?' (Bonhoeffer 1967, 280). So, taking Bonhoeffer's prompt, one way of seeing createdness is as a space that, because of its ordinariness, breaks down barriers between people. That is, the focus is on how we live together in our finite contexts and within the limited goals that these contexts present to us – what does it mean to love our neighbour in the here and now?

This question has a profound political dimension. Not only as a rhetorical challenge for the dynamics of earthly life and its goals, but one that provokes a further question about the creaturely nature of politics itself. Thus, Peter Scott describes creation *ex nihilo* as the 'first political act', an act of freedom, an act of 'letting-be' (Scott 2007, 337). He argues that the doctrine of creation should play a central role in political theology because it 'identifies theological issues central to the truth of human life: What is the creaturely context in which humans (and other kinds) are placed?' (333). Expressing a perspective to which we have already alluded, Scott reflects on the role the doctrine of creation *ex nihilo* might have on political theology and argues that ignoring the doctrine results in too great an emphasis being placed on *redemption* in a purely idealistic sense (333). The crux of his point rests chiefly on the worry that a political theology without the doctrine of creation is 'insufficiently materialist'; but why might we be concerned about this? Because without the reminder of our basic createdness, we enter the unforgiving world of utopian politics. The utopian mind was something opposed by the twentieth century political theorist, Aurel Kolnai (1900–73) who wrote: ' ... Utopia means a tensionless world from which the standard divisions intrinsic to the human condition have been cleared away; a world no longer properly a 'world' in which man is placed but a supra-mundane creation or expansion of man entirely 'at one' with himself.' (Kolnai 1995, 18). So, returning to Scott's point, what the doctrine of creation does is to make political theology less idealistic and more grounded in material and quotidian realities; it directs attention away from excessive utopianism and reminds us of the untidiness of finite life and its true scope. If politics becomes captivated by a transcendent vision, then this may seriously misconstrue the political task of governing human life; but a creational political theology will bring into focus the practical and material ways that people engage each other to address common causes in the world (poverty, injustice) and with human finitude (health and wellbeing) (Scott 2007, 333).

Similarly, if we return to the work of David Kelsey, he argues that the smaller goals of the quotidian (the terrain of the Wisdom literature) are not to be weighed against the larger goals of human perfectionism. By this, he means not so much the eschatological goals of religious faith, but more the oppression of modern utopian metanarratives. One interesting observation that Kelsey makes is that quotidian life cannot be trivialized by death.[15] He writes:

> Unlike the meaning of lives unified as wholes by life-totalizing projects, the meaning of lives engaged in *ad hoc* quotidian projects cannot be undercut by the inevitability of death. The meaning of such lives is grounded on God's creative relating to the quotidian, not on the goal actualized through the projects themselves, a goal that death dissolves (Kelsey 2009, 327–328).

In short, the goals of everyday life have their own integrity without reference to the bigger picture, and perhaps there is an accompanying advantage associated

---

[15] For an extended discussion of Kelsey, see Cheetham 2020, 103–107.

with this: in the absence of the life-totalising scheme, our immediate goals become a valid use of time. The quotidian life does not find itself in the same domain as a theology of *ends,* it does not worry about tomorrow, and if it is a legitimate ingredient in a theological (rather than merely a phenomenological) description of creation then, alongside the bigger narratives about the final consummation of history, we can begin to see the implications about what we can include in a theological description of human action. In fact, createdness is something that is significant to any proper theological anthropology. That is, our created state is not to be put aside or downgraded by an appeal to a higher plane, as if it were a temporary passage towards something that transcends it. Notwithstanding the soteriological hope towards final fulfilment (for example, 'being transformed into the same image from one degree of glory to another' 2. Cor. 3.18), we must also say that createdness is an element of human ontology which begs the acceptance of finitude and limitation. This has profound implications for how we express human hopes and the form that they take. So, to wholeheartedly inhabit createdness implies that the expectation for the so-called human project cannot be solely mapped by metaphysical goals or the 'grand sweep of history'.

Nevertheless, a criticism of this might be that we are limiting our account to a particularly Latin or Augustinian style of thinking. What about voices like Irenaeus or Gregory of Nyssa, who, as we have seen in the last section, present a more developmental vision of human createdness? In fact, one of the core ideas of Eastern Christianity is *theosis,* which denotes the process of humans gradually being transformed into the likeness of God. Although not eschewing creation by any means, there is a vision expressed here not just about what humans do as embodied creatures, but also a hope, or yearning, to ultimately be in union with God. Thus, in his work *You Are Gods: on Nature and Supernature* (2022), David Bentley Hart makes this powerful statement: 'Creation is already deification – is, in fact, theogony' (20). For Hart, our rationality can only make sense in light of the ultimate rationality upon which it depends. Thus, fundamentally, we were made to be deified creatures, and the mind of creation is preoccupied with the Mind that forged it. He thinks that the gaze of human rationality and hope is aimed not at immediate objects but at the transcendent; rationality *compels* this because 'any intellectual predilection toward a merely immediate terminus of longing can be nothing other than a mediating modality and local contraction of a total spiritual volition toward the divine' (Hart 2022, 13). In this sense, then, simply residing in the penultimate space is not the whole story of creation, and in fact, it is misleading to vaunt it any more than is necessary. Again, Hart writes: 'All proximate objects are known to us, and so desired or disregarded or rejected, in light of that anticipated finality' (15).

There is no doubting the powerful spiritual insight in Hart's argument, but is his interpretation of human rational aspirations an over-Platonization? Is the alleged love affair with rationality something that adequately encapsulates the totality of human yearnings (rather than just those of philosophers)? One indication of how Hart intends us to view his argument is perhaps revealed at the beginning of his text where he refers to the advice he received from a colleague about using the sub-title 'Studies in Vedantic Christianity'. This seems entirely apposite to his approach and indicates the alignment of his thinking, but it would be a mistake to dismiss his work as a comparative exercise (it isn't), and Hart's position is an important reminder that a discussion of the penultimate, however exuberant, is about the *pen*ultimate. Creation's ultimate purpose is to fix our eyes on the Creator.

3.1 Gift and Action

Reflecting on creation as a gift, Kenneth Schmitz said: 'The gift, then, is the medium in and through which giver and recipient affirm their being-in-the-world-together. It is the place of celebration of their co-presence' (Schmitz 1982, 81). We should note that here the suggestion is not simply that it is a matter of us opting, as if inspired by the divine gift, to engage in an *imitation* of divine generosity or openness. Instead, there is already an *ontology* of gift underpinning creation and human relationships (see Oliver 2017, 154). It is this giftedness that should be the ground of reparative discourse and action in solidarity with others and the world. Creation as gift acts as a relational equalizer; it implies that we cannot perceive other created beings as mere pawns in our schemes as if we had some *other* justifying status that placed us meritoriously above them: we too are the result of 'gift.'

Nevertheless, what do we do with this gift? Are there any meaningful purposes and activities that we can be engaged with in a world that is an unnecessary creation by a God who is already fully satisfied? So, one of the most significant questions concerns the purpose of human work and its possible role in co-creation. This is an area of some considerable controversy that highlights many of the themes that we have discussed earlier about the dynamics between creation and Creator. Does our work contribute to creation in some way? This is the view taken by John Paul II in *Laborem Exercens* where he writes: 'The Church is convinced that work is a fundamental dimension of man's existence on earth' (John Paul II 2003, 6) and that humanity has the task of transforming the world and by doing so becoming 'more human'. In contrast, Stanley Hauerwas (taking a shot at *Laborem Exercens*) opposes the idea of human beings as co-creators with God: 'Our work does not have to contribute to some grand plan ... ' he writes, and ' ... perhaps most of all, work gives us a way to stay busy' (Hauerwas 1983, 48). For Hauerwas, creation is an act of God alone, and our involvement in it can only be interpreted in terms of grace and surplus. Nevertheless, his position, whilst being strictly consistent with the idea of creation and our own existence as a sheer gift, seems oddly unsatisfying. So, we might challenge this by asking what is being *modelled* by the act of divine creation and if there is a virtue to be found in imitating the divine act of making and engaged activity?

Going further, we could argue that there is something inevitable about the productivity of creation. Take, for example, Augustine's doctrine of *rationes seminales* – the inherent principles that determine the development of living things. The earth 'received the power of bringing them forth', and 'in the roots of time, God created what was to be in times to come' (Augustine 1982, 153). Similarly, Aquinas seeks to show the full integrity of created being, the main principle being 'the perfection of the effect demonstrates the perfection of the cause' (Aquinas 1923b, 15). Creation is not just a passive recipient, on the contrary 'the creature is a moved *mover*' (Webster 2013, 171). To be created out of nothing is no degradation, as if left bereft of any independent validity. On the contrary, for Aquinas, we are given a nature which allows us to achieve great things and contribute some 'great work' to the creation, such a work that befits the *imago dei*.[16]

In this connection, Francis Watson offers a helpful clarification when he discusses two kinds of creation (whilst opting for a third): the speech-act and the fabrication models. The speech-act model reflects an imperative sense of divine command that is exemplified by such biblical passages as Ps. 33.6, which says, 'By the word of the Lord the heavens were made, and all the host by the breath of his mouth.' The fabrication model is concerned with the craftsmanship of the divine creative act, for example, Ps. 139:13: 'For you created my inmost being; you knit me together in my mother's womb ...' However, Watson presents a third model of creation that brings together elements of the speech-act and the fabrication models. Thus, what he calls the 'mediation' model draws attention to the recurring phrase 'Let the earth bring forth ...' (Gen 1:11–24) (See Watson 1994). Here we have a dynamic and active notion of sub-creation, as if the world contains its own agencies to 'bring forth', as permitted or enabled by God. We can perhaps see here the resonance with Augustine's notion of *rationes seminales* above.

One of the big questions that we have already hinted at in connection with David Bentley Hart's portrayal of human rationality as being fixated on the

---

[16] See the conclusion of Webster 2013.

'anticipated finality', is whether there is room for any *local* affections – can the only permissible love be love for God? For example, in his *Summa*, Thomas Aquinas asks, 'does the love which is charity focus solely on God or does it also include our neighbour?' (IIa IIae, 25.1). Aquinas' question is concerned with priority. Since God is the perfect object of love, can true charity only be directed towards the God who is *represented* in our neighbour? Indeed, one might recall Matthew 25:35–40, especially vs 40b: 'Truly I tell you, just as you did it to one of the least of these who are members of my family, you did it to me.' However, for Aquinas, God creates beings that are different from God, and the divine love is therefore directed out of God and towards them. God does not desire to simply stare into a mirror. That is, the movement of divine love towards the creature seeks to preserve the full integrity of that difference. The implication of this is that we too are called to love our neighbour as they are *in themselves* rather than solely the God who we see in them. God is the reason why we love, not the sole object of love. In IIa IIae, 25.4 of the *Summa*, he draws an inference from Leviticus 19:18b that you should 'love your neighbour *as yourself*[17] or for the love of charity itself. Thus, Aquinas' order of charity acknowledges the multiple objects of love in creation, in which he places love for God at the top, but there is also the love of ourselves.

3.2 Gift and Rest

Levenson draws certain parallels between God's rest from his works in Gen 2.2 (or God's *otiosity*, as Levenson calls it) and other similar notions in Near Eastern accounts, but he argues that it has a specific connotation for the Genesis text. Where the Near Eastern gods withdraw, or finish, from their involvement with the world (or become inactive and 'otiose') the Genesis account refers to the 'special form of repose' that we associate with the biblical Sabbath (Levenson 1994, 110). He links Sabbath with 'creation without opposition', such that God's seeming inactivity is not to be seen as a feckless kind of neglect, but rather a positive indication that 'creation is so secure that that it can survive a day without his maintenance.' Thus, we are invited into 'the inner rhythm of creation itself' (111). However, as it is about creation itself, this inner rhythm must apply beyond a solely Jewish liturgical context. Judith Shulevitz observes that the Sabbath 'was the only ritual law among the Ten Commandments, which Christians have held to be universal or natural laws – that is, a kind of innate morality implanted by God in the human soul' (Shulevitz 2010, xxvi). Again, David Burrell argues that the distinctive idea of the Sabbath became obscured over time because of its 'liturgical replacement' by *the day of the Lord,* which

---

[17] See Pohier 1985, 268.See also Williams 1999, chapter 5.

effectively 'invited the community of believers to let redemption eclipse creation' (Burrell 2004, 208). The rabbinical teaching concerning Genesis that the world had been created in good order but that the purpose of humanity was to bring it to completion had obscured the idea of creation as sheer Gift and the Sabbath as a bare invitation into God's rest. Thus, he argues that the very point of the Sabbath is to disabuse humanity from the belief that they are involved in the making of creation.[18] That is, Sabbath returns human beings to their created nature as the mere recipient, rather than architect, of their existence. Similarly, Karl Barth's oft-quoted statement that 'on the Sabbath he [humanity] belongs to himself' refers to the person who, after the six days of work have finished, becomes 'just the man' (Barth 1958, 214). In this vein, might we suppose that the Sabbath time returns humanity to its bare nature, a time without any obligation to fulfil outstanding tasks or commands, a time to just *be*? This places *rest* at the centre of an ethic of createdness and human relationships. The Sabbath-rest is woven into creation itself, and its particular ethic may not serve to end human work necessarily, but to act as a critique of the enslavement to work. (This is the meaning behind Hauerwas' quip we saw earlier about the purpose of work being no more than to 'keep us busy'). Additionally, rather than reading the creation narrative as prioritizing the six 'creative' days – followed by the seventh 'inactive' day (Sabbath), Sabbath-rest is in fact the underlying condition of making. It characterizes the *tone* of creation and the creaturely view: 'The goal of creation . . . is the event of God's Sabbath freedom [. . .] It is *the starting-point for all that follows*' (Barth 1958, 98).[19]

Therefore, to speak of the universality of the Sabbath means that we have to move beyond the cultic aspects and think more metaphysically. The Jewish philosopher, Aristobulus, makes a connection between the seventh day (Sabbath) of creation and the first day (the creation of light). He associates it with philosophical illumination. That is, the seventh day of creation is something given to all of humanity in order for there to be a space to contemplate the light: 'God, who has established the whole cosmos, has also given us as a rest – because life is troublesome for all – the seventh day, which indeed may be called the first also, the creation of light, by which all things can be seen together at the same time' (Mras 2016, 152).

Aristobulus was an Alexandrian (second century CE) and one of the first Jewish thinkers to embrace the allegorical method in Biblical commentary. His purpose in doing this was to show that the Jewish Torah – with all its visceral historicity – could (by the use of allegory) be made compatible with the high

---

[18] The Sabbath invited humanity 'to recognise how the world went on without us and so offering us the opening to return praise to its Creator' (208).

[19] Emphasis mine.

philosophy of the Greeks (Mras 2016, 138–154). He suggested this by giving less attention to the everyday practices of the Sabbath and more to stressing the metaphysics of light and knowledge that might lie at the heart of its meaning. But what does this mean? It is about the conditions that the Sabbath permits – a time of repose and rest, taking time out. Thus, seeing truth and light is made possible by residing inside the gift of divine rest. The meaning here is that the light is not really to be contemplated as the result of arduous human intellectual effort or achievement, but occurs in a moment of amnesty; it is a gift to the sabbatical mind. Creation allows just such a Sabbath.[20] That is, there is a connection being made between Sabbath rest and getting the right perspective and, perhaps, here we might begin to discern a distinctive characteristic about how the Abrahamic notion of a six-day creation by God influences the ways we should regard our human identity as creatures, our relationship to the world, and our sense of the particular rhythms of life. The Protestant theologian, Jürgen Moltmann, champions this when he writes: 'The goal and completion of every Jewish and every Christian doctrine of creation must be the doctrine of the sabbath.' Unlike secular interpretations of the world as *nature* the sabbatical view imbues creation with a particular character: 'it is the sabbath which manifests the world's identity as creation, sanctifies it and blesses it' (Moltmann 1985, 276).

There are also broader lessons to draw according to Shulevitz who remarks that the reason that God rested from his work was to teach us that 'what we create becomes meaningful only once we stop creating it and start remembering why it was worth creating it in the first place [or why it *wasn't*]' (Shulevitz 2010, 217). She offers the view that the practice of the Sabbath by societies is efficacious. It '*does* something' quite remarkable and promotes 'social solidarity' (37). Sabbath rest is quotidian, it occurs in the home, away from human work. It takes place in an activity that is neither urgent nor productive (xxiii). But, if so, such efficacy is not well-described as foundational, as if we might install it as an abstract moral principle, rather, it is *commonplace*. If Sabbath rest can become the basis for embracing the other, it is not because it establishes a common ethic—it is not the Golden Rule—rather it is an invitation to put time on hold, an amnesty where we can be, as Barth said, 'just the man ... whose being and existence are more than all these things and his work' (Barth 1958, 214).

In summary, in this section, we have discussed creation for itself. I would argue that if one rejects the more emanationist or pantheist versions of creation

---

[20] I discuss the relationship between creation and sabbath, and speculate about possible connections to Buddhism, in Cheetham 2020: 85–93.

and chooses the *ex nihilo* model, we not only make room for creation we also permit a far more complex and rich account of the nature of the created life and its goals. This is much more the case if humanity is not simply absorbed by the divine and is not understood to have a being and purpose that can only be wholly synonymous with that identity. Moreover, the autonomy of the human may have some broader or more independent purposes than redemptive or salvific ones. In this sense, the created life is *sui generis*, not just driven by soteriological or transcendent goals, but something unique that includes the complexity of the quotidian and human work. Moreover, the acknowledgement of createdness has political implications – a reminder perhaps of the acceptability of human limitation and the folly of utopianism. Reduced to its barest elements, createdness affirms the vividness of our ordinary experience and the goodness of other loves. It is a sabbatical from the grand totalising projects that are impatient with finite joys and the sheer gift of existence.

Epilogue

In bringing monotheism and creation together in this short book, we have surveyed some (though by no means all) of the models that are offered as an account of this relationship, but have sought to support the mainstream creation *ex nihilo* viewpoint in particular. Perhaps the most obvious consequence of this is that the universe is claimed to have a personal ground, it is not the product of impersonal forces. Nor can it really share much affinity with non-theistic religious accounts that present pantheist visions. Besides, in the latter case, pantheists may be resistant to a 'creation' narrative that is arguably set up on theistic terms and which will presuppose a linear historical story that is illfitting. Furthermore, considering the relationship between God and creation forces us to ask questions about what kind of God is presupposed and what this means for the ontology of creation itself. As we have seen, for feminist writers, the picture presented by creation *ex nihilo* is suggestive of a dominant, powerful God who triumphantly brings things into being from outside. From their perspective, this is an unsympathetic picture that betrays a patriarchal heritage and is unsuited to more empathetic and dynamic models of co-creativity. Similarly, for the process theologians, the God of creation *ex nihilo* is utterly incoherent because of the implications such an idea has for the genuine freedom of creation itself and the ubiquitous experience of horrendous evil. Conversely, for figures like Aquinas, creation requires a conception of God that is the very 'beginning and end' of all things and the cause and source of all being and things. Without this conception, we do not have 'God' at all, but perhaps something that can only be seen as a maximal being at best. However, we have also seen that talking about God as 'simple' (and not composite) and completely self-existent raises questions about the nature of the difference between God and creation as *non-contrastive*. That is, we cannot talk meaningfully in terms of oppositions. Moreover, God does not require creation, it is an unnecessary gift that adds nothing to God. God does not crave better expression *as God* by creation being around or as a result of history being completed. For some, this might be an appalling model that alienates the creator from creation, for others it will be the source of guarantee that 'all shall be well', ultimately.

However, talking about creation as something other than God also makes us ponder the secrets it might hold, both for understanding ourselves and the divine. On the one hand, our finite understanding can only draw a negative conclusion as the most devastating counter-experiences that creation exhibits is the problem of evil. We see how significant this is in some of the different accounts of creation we have surveyed. Put in this strongest sense, this counter-experience provides grounds for atheism. On the other hand, perhaps creation itself provides us with a key? There is the possibility that looking at creation itself, rather than at transcendent or rational archetypes, paradoxically gives grounds for a more appropriate response to our negative experiences. Creation changes our focus and redirects our thinking into the midst of things, and seeks to draw out a wisdom that is not prone to find a pristine, unmalleable explanations. Of all the Wisdom texts in the Bible, the book of Job stands out as a powerful example of this. So, in the face of intractable questions, the narrative of Job:38–43 directs Job *towards* rather than away from creation in order to present a revelation about the nature, power, and sheer glory of the divine character. That is, creation, rather than being an obstruction, becomes the proper conduit for knowledge of the divine and the mystery of existence. The sheer cumulative impact of these revelations given to Job is to see the glory of plenitude and mystery. The Book of Job provides its spiritual lesson through a doxology of created marvels rather than the rationalism of the theodicist. Furthermore, it draws us into a particular world of finite splendours and blessed limitations that are the deliberate framework for the more 'sabbatical' minds that are content with not being divine.

Interpreting Job, David Ford observes that '[e]ven as we turn from one created phenomenon to another we are not given any overview but one vivid particular after another'. Further, 'the world is a manifold of intensities, each with its created integrity and even untameable wildness' (Ford 2007, 114). It is significant that God's reply at the end of Job acts as a warning to theodicists, not only to Job's comforters contained in the book itself, but perhaps to all those who would seek to provide an explanation of suffering and evil. God rebukes those who would attempt it (Job 42:7–10). However, what is perhaps important to understand is that the Job narrative not only tells a story concerning unfathomable evil but also suggestive of the ways in which these issues are appropriately addressed. The Book of Job presents Job's predicament as an outrageous dissonance that appears incompatible with a just God, but it is not quite accurate to say that Job offers no satisfactory response to suffering and evil. In a way, the story does provide a far more appropriate response by virtue of its refusal to supply an explanatory or transcendent scheme. Instead, it reorients our perspective to learn from what creation reveals, and it delivers a bewildering sense of grandeur, marvel, and excess. It does not take the form of the systematic theological solution, rather we are directed towards a creation which, because of its particularity and wildness, leaves us with a surplus of responses and meanings. This surplus presents an opportunity for the person who is seeking to speak adequately to their fellow creatures about God. In the Book of Job, creation is used to provide illumination by way of a full immersion into the inscrutable excess that it displays. It does not willingly repay attempts at transcendent explanations, instead, it offers 'vivid particularities'. The question is if we can readily inhabit our createdness when it comes to dealing with other theological problems? Is such an approach obviously insufficient or incomplete?

So, finally, in what ways does monotheism *reveal* creation? Looking at some of the options, we have noted that emanationist or pantheist views reveal creation to be part of eternity or infused with the divinity itself. A feminist perspective like Keller's reveals creation to be a place of vital rhythmic creativity possessed with fluctuating possibilities that are becoming 'self-organizing systems' due to the interplay between God and the *tehomic* depths. Similarly, process thinking presents God not as the Absolute but as the 'chief exemplification' of metaphysical principles in order to allow the creation to be a place of freedom and negotiated progression. However powerful these viewpoints are, and however attentive they appear to be to the frailties of human existence, there remains the question of the value of creation apart from divine involvement or constant tinkering. By this, we mean the value of creation apart from any *bigger* project (however theologically infused) designed to take it from one stage to the next, or to assume that it is only partly finished and is involved in its own moulding towards a greater good. For creation to revel in its finitude and wildness, there is something that needs to be said about its inherent goodness as it is. As we said at the beginning, the creation *ex nihilo* picture advances the view that God, self-existent, without need or resistance, created a world without opposition, which added nothing to God, from absolutely nothing. I would argue that it is this that reveals creation as *finite* and not divine and, being intended, this finitude and limitation are somehow vital aspects of its created glory. When discussing pantheism earlier, we noted Austin Farrer's concern about the apparent 'illusion of finite substance' that it implies if all things are subsumed into the infinite. So, if we think that asserting the reality of the finite world is important, then we end up accepting a more standard metaphysical ordering that separates finite from infinite. Perhaps this standard metaphysical ordering, the separation of finite from infinite, is actually a good thing.

References

Agamben, Georgio (2011). *Kingdom and the Glory*. Stanford: Stanford University Press.

Aquinas, Thomas (1996). *Commentary on the Book of Causes of St. Thomas Aquinas*. Translation by Vincent A. Guagliardo, Charles R. Hess, and Richard C. Taylor. Washington, DC: The Catholic University of America Press.

Aquinas, Thomas (1923a). *Summa Contra Gentiles: The Second Book*. London: Burns, Oates and Washbourne.

Aquinas, Thomas (1923b). *Summa Contra Gentiles: The Third Book*. London: Burns, Oates and Washbourne.

Attridge, Harold (1989). *The Epistle to the Hebrews: A Commentary*. Edited by Helmut Koester. Philadelphia: Fortress Press.

Augustine (2003). *City of God*, Book XI.10. Translated by Henry Bettenson. London: Penguin.

Augustine (1995). De natura et gratia. In Alister McGrath (ed.) *The Christian Theology Reader*. Oxford: Blackwells.

Augustine (1982). *The Literal Meaning of Genesis Vol. 1*. Translated by John H. Taylor, S. J. New York:Newman Press.

Barth, Karl (1958). *Church Dogmatics III*. Edited by Geoffrey Bromiley and Thomas Torrance. Edinburgh: T and T Clark.

Bonhoeffer, Dietrich (1997). *Creation and Fall*. Minneapolis: Fortress Press.

Bonhoeffer, Dietrich (1967). *Letters and Papers: Enlarged Edition*, edited by Eberhard Bethge, translated by Reginald Fuller. London: SCM Press.

Brierley, Michael (2004). Naming a Quiet Revolution: The Panentheistic Turn in Modern Theology. In Philip Clayton and Arthur Peacocke (eds.), *In Whom We Live and Move and Have Our Being*. Grand Rapids: Eerdmans, pp. 1–15.

Burrell, David (1979). *Aquinas: God and action*. London: Routledge and Kegan Paul.

Burrell, David (2013). Creatio Ex Nihilo Recovered. *Modern theology*, 29/2, pp. 5–21.

Burrell, David (2004). *Faith and Freedom: An Interfaith Perspective*. Oxford: Wiley-Blackwell.

Burrell, David (1994). *Freedom and Creation in Three Traditions*. Notre Dame: University of Notre Dame Press.

Cheetham, David (2020). *Creation and Religious Pluralism*. Oxford: Oxford University Press.

References

Cheetham, David (2016). *Ways of Meeting and the Theology of Religions*. London: Routledge.

Clayton, Philip (2001). Panentheist Internalism. *Dialog: A Journal of Theology*, 40/3, pp. 208–215.

Clayton, Philip (2011). Panentheism. In Ian McFarland, Karen Kilby, David Fergusson and Iain Torrance (eds.), *Cambridge Dictionary of Christian Theology*. Cambridge: Cambridge University Press, pp. 365–367.

Clifford, Richard (2021). *Creatio ex nihilo* in the Old Testament/Hebrew Bible. In Gary A. Anderson and Markus Bockmuehl (eds.), *Creation ex nihilo: Origins, Development, Contemporary Challenges*. Indiana: University of Notre Dame Press, pp. 55–76.

Cohen, Hermann (1995). *Religion of Reason: Out of the Sources of Judaism*. Translated by Simon Kaplan. Atlanta: Scholars Press.

Davies, Oliver (2004). *The Creativity of God: World, Eucharist, Reason*. Cambridge: Cambridge University Press.

Desmond, William (2005). *Is There a Sabbath for Thought? Between Religion and Philosophy*. New York: Fordham University Press.

Farrer, Austin (1959). *Finite and Infinite: A Philosophical Essay*, 2nd ed. London: Dacre Press.

Ford, David (2007). *Christian Wisdom: Desiring God and Learning in Love*. Cambridge: Cambridge University Press.

Gregerson, Niels (2004). Three Varieties of Pantheism. In Philip Clayton and Arthur Peacocke (eds.), *In Whom We Live and Move and Have Our Being*. Grand Rapids: Eerdmans, pp. 19–35.

Griffin, David (1981). Creation out of Nothing, Creation out of Chaos, and the Problem of Evil. In Stephen Davis (ed.), *Encountering Evil: Live Options in Theodicy*. Edinburgh: T. & T. Clark, pp. 108–124.

Gunton, Colin (1997). The Doctrine of Creation. In Colin Gunton (ed.), *The Cambridge Companion to Christian Doctrine*. Cambridge: Cambridge University Press, pp. 141–157.

Gunton, Colin (2002). *The Christian Faith: An Introduction to Christian Doctrine*. Oxford: Blackwell.

Hardy, David (2003). Creation and Eschatology. In Colin Gunton (ed.), *The Doctrine of Creation: Essays in Dogmatics, History and Philosophy*. London: T&T Clark, pp. 105–134.

Hart, David Bentley (2003). *The Beauty of the Infinite: The Aesthetics of Christian Truth*. Grand Rapids: Eerdmans.

Hart, David Bentley (2019). *That All Shall Be Saved*. New Haven: Yale University Press.

Hart, David Bentley (2022). *You Are Gods: On Nature and Supernatural*. Notre Dame: University of Notre Dame Press.

Hauerwas, Stanley (1983). Work as Co-Creation: a Critique of a Remarkably Bad Idea. In John W. Houck and Oliver F. Williams, (eds.) *Co-Creation and Capitalism: John Paul II's Laborem Exercens*. Washington: University Press of America, pp. 42–58.

Heschel, Abraham (1951). *The Sabbath: It's Meaning for Modern Man*. New York: Farrar, Straus and Giroux.

Hick, John (2007 [1966]). *Evil and the God of Love*. Basingstoke: Palgrave Macmillan.

Irenaeus (1990). *Adversus Haereses*, IV. Xxxviii.2–3 in H. Bettenson, editor and translator, *The Early Christian Fathers*. Oxford: Oxford University Press.

Irenaeus, Dominic (2012). *Against the Heresies, Book 2*. Translated by D. J Unger, (revised by D. J Dhillon). New York: The Newman Press.

Jenson, Robert (2004). Aspects of a Doctrine of Creation. In Colin Gunton (ed.), *The Doctrine of Creation: Essays in Dogmatics, History and Philosophy*. London: T&T Clark, pp. 17–28.

John Paul II (2003). *Laborem Exercens*. London: Pauline Books & Media.

Keller, Catherine (2003). *The Face of the Deep: A Theology of Becoming*. Abingdon: Routledge.

Kelsey, David (2009). *Eccentric Existence: A Theological Anthropology*. Louisville: Westminster John Knox.

Kierkegaard, Soren (1992). *Concluding Unscientific Postscript*. Edited and translated by Howard V. Hong and Edna H. Hong. Princeton: Princeton University Press.

Kierkegaard, Soren (2012). *The Essential Kierkegaard*. Edited and translated by Edna H. Hong and Howard V. Hong. Princeton: Princeton University Press.

Kolnai, Aurel (1995). *The Utopian Mind and Other Papers*, Edited by F. Dunlop. London: Athlone Press.

Krauss, Lawrence M. (2012). *A Universe from Nothing: Why There Is Something Rather Than Nothing*. New York: Free Press.

Leidenhag, Joanna (2020). *Creation and Ecology: Why the Doctrine of Creation ex nihilo Matters Today*. Cambridge: Grove Books.

Leidenhag, Joanna (2021). *Minding Creation: Theological Panpsychism and the Doctrine of Creation*. Edinburgh: T&T Clark.

Levenson, Jon (1994). *Creation and the Persistence of Evil: The Jewish Drama of Divine Omnipotence*. Princeton: Princeton University Press.

Levering, Matthew (2017). *Engaging the Doctrine of Creation: Cosmos, Creatures and the Wise and Good Creator*. Grand Rapids: Baker Academic.

Levine, Michael (1994). *Pantheism: A non-theistic concept of deity.* London: Routledge.

Louth, Andrew (2020). Book Review: *That All Shall Be Saved: Heaven, Hell and Universal Salvation* by David Bentley Hart. *Journal of Orthodox Christian Studies*, 3/2, p. 235.

May, Gerhard (2006). Monotheism and Creation. In M. M. Mitchell and F. M. Young (eds.), *Cambridge History of Christianity Vol.1.* Cambridge: Cambridge University Press, pp. 434–451.

McFague, Sallie (1987). *Models of God: Theology for an Ecological Nuclear Age.* London: SCM Press.

McFarland, Ian (2014). *From Nothing: A Theology of Creation.* Louisville: Westminster John Knox Press.

McRandal, Janice (2015). *Christian Doctrine and the Grammar or Difference.* Minneapolis: Fortress Press.

Merleau-Ponty, Maurice (2012 [1945]). *Phenomenology of Perception.* Translated by Donald A. Landes. London: Routledge.

Moltmann, Jürgen (1985). *God and Creation: An Ecological Doctrine of Creation.* London: SCM Press.

Mras (ed.). (2016). *Eusebius Werke.* Bd.8: *Die Praeparatio Evangelica* (GCS, 43, 1–2) in de Vos, 'Aristobulus and the Universal Sabbath'. In George Brooke and Pierre van Hecke (eds.), *Goochem in Mokum, Wisdom in Amsterdam.* Leiden: Brill, pp. 138–154.

Norris, Richard (1966). *God and World in Early Christian Theology: A Study of Justin Martyr, Irenaeus, Tertullian and Origen.* London: Adam and Charles Black.

O'Shaughnessy, Thomas (1985). Creation and the Teaching of the Qur'ān. Rome: Biblical Institute Press.

Oliver, Simon (2017). *Creation: A Guide for the Perplexed.* London: Bloomsbury.

Philo (1989). De Mutatione nominum. 4.27, in *Philo - Volume V, Loeb Classical Library.* Translated by Francis H. Colson and George H. Whitaker. Cited in Soskice, Why *Creatio ex nihilo* for Theology Today?, Cambridge: Harvard University Press, p. 53.

Pieper, Josef (1957). *The Silence of St Thomas: Three Essays.* Translated by Daniel O'Connor. London: Faber and Faber.

Plato (1892). *The Dialogues of Plato Vol 3: The Timaeus.* Translation by Benjamin Jowett. Oxford: Clarendon Press.

Plotinus (1984). *Ennead V.* Translation by Arthur H. Armstrong. London: Heinemann.

Pohier, Jacques (1985). *Dieu Fractures* (Paris: Editions de Seuil, 1985). Translated by John Bowden, *God in Fragments*. London: SCM Press.

Schillebeeckx, Edward (1990). *Church: The Human Story of God*. London: SCM Press.

Schillebeeckx, Edward (1982). *Interim Report on the Books Jesus and Christ*. Trans. John Bowden. New York: Crossroad.

Schmitz, Kenneth (1982). *The Gift: Creation*. Milwaukee: Marquette University Press.

Schopenhauer, Arthur (1974) [1851]. *Parerga and Paralipomena*. Translated by Eric F. J. Payne, Oxford: Clarendon.

Schopenhauer, Arthur (2008). *World as Will and Representation*. Vols. 1 & 2. Translated by Richard Aquila and David Corus. London: Pearson Longman.

Schwöbel, Christoph (2004). God, Creation and Christian Community: The Dogmatic Basis for a Christian Ethics of Createdness. In Colin Gunton (ed.), *The Doctrine of Creation*. London: T&T Clark, pp. 149–176.

Scott, Peter (2007). Creation. In Peter Scott and William T. Cavanaugh (eds.), *The Blackwell Companion to Political Theology*. Oxford: Blackwell, pp. 333–347.

Shulevitz, Judith (2010). *The Sabbath World: Glimpses of a Different Order of Time*. New York: Random House.

Sokolowski, Robert (1982). *The God of Faith and Reason: Foundations of Christian Theology*. Notre Dame: University of Notre Dame Press.

Soskice, Janet (2021). In Why *Creatio ex nihilo* for Theology Today? In Gary A. Anderson and Markus Bockmuehl (eds.), *Creation ex nihilo: Origins, Development, Contemporary Challenges*. Indiana: University of Notre Dame Press, pp. 37–54.

Stenmark, Mikael (2019). Panentheism and its Neighbours. *International Journal for Philosophy of Religion*, 85, 23–41.

Tanner, Kathryn (1988). *God and Creation in Christian Theology*. Minneapolis: Fortress Press.

Theophilus of Antioch (1970). *Ad Autolycum*. Text and translation by Robert M. Grant. Oxford: Clarendon Press.

Torrance, Alan (2004). *Creatio ex nihilo* and the Spatio-Temporal Dimensions, with special reference to Jürgen Moltmann and D. C. Williams. In Colin Gunton (ed.), *The Doctrine of Creation: Essays in Dogmatics, History and Philosophy*. Edinburgh: T&T Clark, pp. 83–103.

Tweed, Thomas (2015). After the Quotidian Turn: Interpretive Categories and Scholarly Trajectories in the Study of Religion since the 1960s. *Journal of Religion*, 95/3, pp. 361–385.

Vail, Eric (2012). *Creation and Chaos Talk: Charting a Way Forward*. Eugene: Pickwick.

Ward, Keith (2004). The World as the Body of God: A Panentheistic Metaphor. In Philip Clayton and Arthur Peacocke (eds.), *In Whom We Live and Move and Have Our Being*. Grand Rapids: Eerdmans, pp. 62–72.

Watson, Francis (1994). *Text, Church and World: Biblical Interpretation in Theological Perspective*. Edinburgh: T. & T. Clark.

Webster, John (2013). Love Is also a Lover of Life: *Creatio Ex Nihilo* and Creaturely Goodness. *Modern Theology*, 29/2, pp. 156–171.

Weeks, Stuart (2016). The Place and Limit of Wisdom Revisited. In John Jarick (ed.), *Perspectives on Israelite Wisdom*. London: Continuum, pp. 3–23.

White, Lynn (1967). The Historical Roots of Our Ecological Crisis. *Science*, 155/3767, pp. 1203–1207.

Whitehead, Alfred (1978). *Process and Reality: An Essay in Cosmology* Corrected, Edited by David R. Griffin and Donald W. Sherburne. New York: Free Press.

Williams, Rowan (2016). *On Augustine*. London: Bloomsbury.

Williams, Rowan (1999). *On Christian Theology*. Oxford: Wiley-Blackwell.

Wilson, Jonathan (2013). *God's Good World: Reclaiming the Doctrine of Creation*. Grand Rapids: Baker Academic.

Zimmerli, Walther (1964). The Place and Limit of the Wisdom in the Framework of the Old Testament Theology. *Scottish Journal of Theology*, 17/2, pp. 146–158.

Acknowledgement

My thanks to Oxford University Press for permission to rework some short sections from Cheetham, 2020.

About the Author

David Cheetham is Professor of Philosophical Theology at the University of Birmingham, UK. He has published widely in the fields of the philosophy of religion, contemporary theology, religion and aesthetics. His publications include *John Hick* (Routledge 2016) and *Creation and Religious Pluralism: A Christian Theology* (Oxford, 2020).

Cambridge Elements

Religion and Monotheism

Paul K. Moser
Loyola University Chicago

Paul K. Moser is Professor of Philosophy at Loyola University Chicago. He is the author of *God in Moral Experience; Paul's Gospel of Divine Self-Sacrifice; The Divine Goodness of Jesus; Divine Guidance; Understanding Religious Experience; The God Relationship; The Elusive God* (winner of national book award from the Jesuit Honor Society); *The Evidence for God; The Severity of God; Knowledge and Evidence* (all Cambridge University Press); and *Philosophy after Objectivity* (Oxford University Press); coauthor of *Theory of Knowledge* (Oxford University Press); editor of *Jesus and Philosophy* (Cambridge University Press) and *The Oxford Handbook of Epistemology* (Oxford University Press); and coeditor of *The Wisdom of the Christian Faith* (Cambridge University Press). He is the coeditor with Chad Meister of the book series *Cambridge Studies in Religion, Philosophy, and Society*.

Chad Meister
Affiliate Scholar, Ansari Institute for Global Engagement with Religion, University of Notre Dame

Chad Meister is Affiliate Scholar at the Ansari Institute for Global Engagement with Religion at the University of Notre Dame. His authored and co-authored books include *Evil: A Guide for the Perplexed* (Bloomsbury Academic, 2nd edition); *Introducing Philosophy of Religion* (Routledge); *Introducing Christian Thought* (Routledge, 2nd edition); and *Contemporary Philosophical Theology* (Routledge). He has edited or co-edited the following: *The Oxford Handbook of Religious Diversity* (Oxford University Press); *Debating Christian Theism* (Oxford University Press); with Paul Moser, *The Cambridge Companion to the Problem of Evil* (Cambridge University Press); and with Charles Taliaferro, *The History of Evil* (Routledge, in six volumes). He is the co-editor with Paul Moser of the book series *Cambridge Studies in Religion, Philosophy, and Society*.

About the Series

This Cambridge Element series publishes original concise volumes on monotheism and its significance. Monotheism has occupied inquirers since the time of the Biblical patriarch, and it continues to attract interdisciplinary academic work today. Engaging, current, and concise, the Elements benefit teachers, researched, and advanced students in religious studies, Biblical studies, theology, philosophy of religion, and related fields.

Cambridge Elements

Religion and Monotheism

Elements in the Series

Monotheism and Religious Experience
Mark Owen Webb

Music and Monotheism
Gareth F. Wilson

Jewish Concepts of Divine Oneness: A Comparative Introduction
Job Y. Jindo

The Politics of Monotheism
Ragnar M. Bergem

Angels and Monotheism
Michael D. Hurley

Monotheism and Paradise
Caitlin Smith Gilson

Monotheism and Miracle
Eric Eve

Monotheism and Peacebuilding
John D Brewer

Monotheism and Relativism
Bernd Irlenborn

Monotheism and Wisdom in the Hebrew Bible: An Uneasy Pair?
James L. Crenshaw

Seeking Monotheism in Chinese Religions
Huaiyu Chen

Monotheism and Creation
David Cheetham

A full series listing is available at: www.cambridge.org/er&m

For EU product safety concerns, contact us at Calle de José Abascal, 56–1°,
28003 Madrid, Spain or eugpsr@cambridge.org.

www.ingramcontent.com/pod-product-compliance
Lightning Source LLC
LaVergne TN
LVHW011858060526
838200LV00054B/4411